Beck Jacks

Specialty Guidelines
for the Delivery of Services

Clinical Psychologists
Counseling Psychologists
Industrial/Organizational Psychologists
School Psychologists

Committee on Professional Standards,
American Psychological Association

American Psychological Association
Washington, D.C.

Reprinted from the *American Psychologist,* June 1981, Vol. 36, No. 6, pp. 640-681.
Copyright © 1981 by the American Psychological Association.
ISBN: 0-912704-41-1

Contents

Introduction

In September 1976, the APA Council of Representatives reviewed and commented on the draft revisions of the *Standards for Providers of Psychological Services* prepared by the Committee on Standards for Providers of Psychological Services. During that discussion, the Council acknowledged the need for standards in certain specialty areas in addition to the generic *Standards* covered by the draft revision. The Council authorized the committee to hold additional meetings to develop multiple standards in all specialty areas of psychology.

Following the adoption of the revised generic *Standards* in January 1977, the committee, working with psychologists in the four recognized specialty areas of psychology, spent the next three years modifying the generic *Standards* to meet the needs of clinical, counseling, industrial/organizational, and school psychologists. The four documents produced by the committee went through extensive revisions. Convention programs discussing these developments were held every year. Comments were solicited from all major constituencies in psychology and from thousands of individuals. The comments received and reviewed by the committee were varied and numerous.

In January 1980, following this extensive process and after making several additional modifications, the Council of Representatives adopted as APA policy the *Specialty Guidelines for the Delivery of Services by Clinical (Counseling, Industrial/Organizational, School) Psychologists.* As stated in the introductions of these four documents, the intent of the *Specialty Guidelines* is "to educate the public, the profession, and other interested parties regarding specialty professional practices . . . and to facilitate the continued systematic development of the profession."

At the same meeting, the Council also approved a reorganization of the Board of Professional Affairs' committee structure, which included the establishment of the Committee on Professional Standards to succeed the Committee on Standards for Providers of Psychological Services. The Committee on Professional Standards has been directed to review all comments on the *Specialty Guidelines* when considering its revisions. APA members and other interested individuals or groups with comments or suggestions are requested to send them to the American Psychological Association, Committee on Professional Standards, 1200 Seventeenth Street, N.W., Washington, D.C. 20036.

The members of the Committee on Standards for Providers of Psychological Services (1977–1980) who developed the *Specialty Guidelines* were Jack I. Bardon, school; Jules Barron, clinical; Frank Friedlander, industrial/organizational; Morris Goodman, clinical; Durand F. Jacobs (Chair), institutional practice; Barbara A. Kirk, counseling; Nadine M. Lambert, school; Virginia Ellen Schein, industrial/organizational; and Milton Schwebel, counseling. Arthur Centor and Richard Kilburg were the Central Office liaisons.

The members of the Committee on Professional Standards (1980–1981) who made the final changes to the *Specialty Guidelines* and were charged with future revisions were Juanita Braddock, public member; Lorraine Eyde, industrial/organizational; Morris Goodman, clinical; Judy Hall, experimental/mental retardation; John H. Jackson, school; Nadine M. Lambert, school; Dave Mills (1981 Chair, partial), clinical/counseling; Milton Schwebel, counseling; Gilfred Tanabe (1980 Chair), clinical; and Murphy Thomas (1981 Chair, partial), clinical. The Central Office liaisons were Joy Burke, Sharon A. Shueman, and Pam Arnold.

Specialty Guidelines for the Delivery of Services by Clinical Psychologists

The Specialty Guidelines that follow are based on the generic *Standards for Providers of Psychological Services* originally adopted by the American Psychological Association (APA) in September 1974 and revised in January 1977 (APA, 1974b, 1977b). Together with the generic *Standards*, these Specialty Guidelines state the official policy of the Association regarding delivery of services by clinical psychologists. Admission to the practice of psychology is regulated by state statute. It is the position of the Association that licensing be based on generic, and not on specialty, qualifications. Specialty guidelines serve the additional purpose of providing potential users and other interested groups with essential information about particular services available from the several specialties in professional psychology.

Professional psychology specialties have evolved from generic practice in psychology and are supported by university training programs. There are now at least four recognized professional specialties—clinical, counseling, school, and industrial/organizational psychology.

The knowledge base in each of these specialty areas has increased, refining the state of the art to the point that a set of uniform specialty guidelines is now possible and desirable. The present Guidelines are intended to educate the public, the profession, and other interested parties regarding specialty professional practices. They are also intended to facilitate the continued systematic development of the profession.

The content of each Specialty Guideline reflects a consensus of university faculty and public and private practitioners regarding the knowledge base, services provided, problems addressed, and clients served.

Traditionally, all learned disciplines have treated the designation of specialty practice as a reflection of preparation in greater depth in a particular subject matter, together with a voluntary limiting of focus to a more restricted area of practice by the professional. Lack of specialty designation does not preclude general providers of psychological services from using the methods or dealing with the populations of any specialty, except insofar as psychologists voluntarily refrain from providing services they are not trained to render. It is the intent of these Guidelines, however, that after the grandparenting period, psychologists not put themselves forward as *specialists* in a given area of practice unless they meet the qualifications noted in the Guidelines (see Definitions). Therefore, these Guidelines are meant to apply only to those psychologists who voluntarily wish to be designated as *clinical psychologists*. They do not apply to other psychologists.

These Guidelines represent the profession's best judgment of the conditions, credentials, and experience that contribute to competent professional practice. The APA strongly encourages, and plans to participate in, efforts to identify professional practitioner behaviors and job functions and to validate the relation between these and desired client outcomes. Thus, future revisions of these Guidelines will increasingly reflect the results of such efforts.

These Guidelines follow the format and, wherever applicable, the wording of the generic *Standards*.[1] (Note: Footnotes appear at the end of the Specialty Guidelines. See pp. 648–651.) The intent of these Guidelines is to improve the quality, effectiveness, and accessibility of psychological services. They are meant to provide guidance to providers, users, and sanctioners regarding the best judgment of the profession on these matters. Although the Specialty Guidelines have been derived from and are consistent with the generic *Standards*, they may be used as separate documents. However, *Standards for Providers of Psychological Services* (APA, 1977b) shall remain the basic policy statement and shall take precedence where there are questions of interpretation.

Professional psychology in general and clinical psychology as a specialty have labored long and diligently to codify a uniform set of guidelines for the delivery of services by clinical psychologists that would serve the respective needs of users, providers, third-party purchasers, and sanctioners of psychological services.

The Committee on Professional Standards, established by the APA in January 1980, is charged with keeping the generic *Standards* and the Specialty Guidelines responsive to the needs of the public and the profession. It is also charged with continually reviewing, modifying, and extending them progressively as the profession and the science of psychology develop new knowledge, improved methods, and additional modes of psychological services.

The Specialty Guidelines for the Delivery of Services by Clinical Psychologists that follow have been established by the APA as a means of self-regulation to protect the public interest. They guide the specialty practice of

These Specialty Guidelines were prepared through the cooperative efforts of the APA Committee on Standards for Providers of Psychological Services (COSPOPS) and many professional clinical psychologists from the divisions of APA, including those involved in education and training programs and in public and private practice. Jules Barron, succeeded by Morris Goodman, served as the clinical psychology representative on COSPOPS. The committee was chaired by Durand F. Jacobs; the Central Office liaisons were Arthur Centor and Richard Kilburg.

clinical psychology by specifying important areas of quality assurance and performance that contribute to the goal of facilitating more effective human functioning.

Principles and Implications of the Specialty Guidelines

These Specialty Guidelines have emerged from and reaffirm the same basic principles that guided the development of the generic *Standards for Providers of Psychological Services* (APA, 1977b):

1. These Guidelines recognize that admission to the practice of psychology is regulated by state statute.

2. It is the intention of the APA that the generic *Standards* provide appropriate guidelines for statutory licensing of psychologists. In addition, although it is the position of the APA that licensing be generic and not in specialty areas, these Specialty Guidelines in clinical psychology provide an authoritative reference for use in credentialing specialty providers of clinical psychological services by such groups as divisions of the APA and state associations and by boards and agencies that find such criteria useful for quality assurance.

3. A uniform set of Specialty Guidelines governs the quality of services to all users of clinical psychological services in both the private and the public sectors. Those receiving clinical psychological services are protected by the same kinds of safeguards, irrespective of sector; these include constitutional guarantees, statutory regulation, peer review, consultation, record review, and supervision.

4. A uniform set of Specialty Guidelines governs clinical psychological service functions offered by clinical psychologists, regardless of setting or form of remuneration. All clinical psychologists in professional practice recognize and are responsive to a uniform set of Specialty Guidelines, just as they are guided by a common code of ethics.

5. Clinical psychology Guidelines establish clearly articulated levels of quality for covered clinical psychological service functions, regardless of the nature of the users, purchasers, or sanctioners of such covered services.

6. All persons providing clinical psychological services meet specified levels of training and experience that are consistent with, and appropriate to, the functions they perform. Clinical psychological services provided by persons who do not meet the APA qualifications for a professional clinical psychologist (see Definitions) are supervised by a professional clinical psychologist. Final responsibility and accountability for services provided rest with professional clinical psychologists.

7. When providing any of the covered clinical psychological service functions at any time and in any setting, whether public or private, profit or nonprofit, clinical psychologists observe these Guidelines in order to promote the best interests and welfare of the users of such services. The extent to which clinical psychologists observe these Guidelines is judged by peers.

8. These Guidelines, while assuring the user of the clinical psychologist's accountability for the nature and quality of services specified in this document, do not preclude the clinical psychologist from using new methods or developing innovative procedures in the delivery of clinical services.

These Specialty Guidelines have broad implications both for users of clinical psychological services and for providers of such services:

1. Guidelines for clinical psychological services provide a foundation for mutual understanding between provider and user and facilitate more effective evaluation of services provided and outcomes achieved.

2. Guidelines for clinical psychologists are essential for uniformity in specialty credentialing of clinical psychologists.

3. Guidelines give specific content to the profession's concept of ethical practice as it applies to the functions of clinical psychologists.

4. Guidelines for clinical psychological services may have significant impact on tomorrow's education and training models for both professional and support personnel in clinical psychology.

5. Guidelines for the provision of clinical psychological services in human service facilities influence the determination of acceptable structure, budgeting, and staffing patterns in these facilities.

6. Guidelines for clinical psychological services require continual review and revision.

The Specialty Guidelines here presented are intended to improve the quality and delivery of clinical psychological services by specifying criteria for key aspects of the practice setting. Some settings may require additional and/or more stringent criteria for specific areas of service delivery.

Systematically applied, these Guidelines serve to establish a more effective and consistent basis for evaluating the performance of individual service providers as well as to guide the organization of clinical psychological service units in human service settings.

Definitions

Providers of clinical psychological services refers to two categories of persons who provide clinical psychological services:

A. Professional clinical psychologists.[2] Professional clinical psychologists have a doctoral degree from a regionally accredited university or professional school providing an organized, sequential clinical psychology program in a department of psychology in a university or college, or in an appropriate department or unit of a professional school. Clinical psychology programs that are accredited by the American Psychological Association are recognized as meeting the definition of a clinical psychology program. Clinical psychology programs that are not accredited by the American Psychological Association meet the definition of a clinical psychology program if they satisfy the following criteria:

1. The program is primarily psychological in nature and stands as a recognizable, coherent 'organizational entity within the institution.

2. The program provides an integrated, organized sequence of study.

3. The program has an identifiable body of students who are matriculated in that program for a degree.

4. There is a clear authority with primary responsibility for the core and specialty areas, whether or not the program cuts across administrative lines.

5. There is an identifiable psychology faculty, and a psychologist is responsible for the program.

In addition to a doctoral education, clinical psychologists acquire doctoral and postdoctoral training. Patterns of education and training in clinical psychology[3] are consistent with the functions to be performed and the services to be provided, in accordance with the ages, populations, and problems encountered in various settings.

B. All other persons who are not professional clinical psychologists and who participate in the delivery of clinical psychological services under the supervision of a professional clinical psychologist. Although there may be variations in the titles of such persons, they are not referred to as clinical psychologists. Their functions may be indicated by use of the adjective *psychological* preceding the noun, for example, *psychological associate, psychological assistant, psychological technician*, or *psychological aide*. Their services are rendered under the supervision of a professional clinical psychologist, who is responsible for the designation given them and for quality control. To be assigned such a designation, a person has the background, training, or experience that is appropriate to the functions performed.

Clinical psychological services refers to the application of principles, methods, and procedures for understanding, predicting, and alleviating intellectual, emotional, psychological, and behavioral disability and discomfort. Direct services are provided in a variety of health settings, and direct and supportive services are provided in the entire range of social, organizational, and academic institutions and agencies.[4] Clinical psychological services include the following:[5]

A. Assessment directed toward diagnosing the nature and causes, and predicting the effects, of subjective distress; of personal, social, and work dysfunction; and of the psychological and emotional factors involved in, and consequent to, physical disease and disability. Procedures may include, but are not limited to, interviewing, and administering and interpreting tests of intellectual abilities, attitudes, emotions, motivations, personality characteristics, psychoneurological status, and other aspects of human experience and behavior relevant to the disturbance.

B. Interventions directed at identifying and correcting the emotional conflicts, personality disturbances, and skill deficits underlying a person's distress and/or dysfunction. Interventions may reflect a variety of theoretical orientations, techniques, and modalities. These may include, but are not limited to, psychotherapy, psychoanalysis, behavior therapy, marital and family therapy, group psychotherapy, hypnotherapy, social-learning approaches, biofeedback techniques, and environmental consultation and design.

C. Professional consultation in relation to A and B above.

D. Program development services in the areas of A, B, and C above.

E. Supervision of clinical psychological services.

F. Evaluation of all services noted in A through E above.

A *clinical psychological service unit* is the functional unit through which clinical psychological services are provided; such a unit may be part of a larger psychological service organization comprising psychologists of more than one specialty and headed by a professional psychologist:

A. A clinical psychological service unit provides predominantly clinical psychological services and is composed of one or more professional clinical psychologists and supporting staff.

B. A clinical psychological service unit may operate as a professional service or as a functional or geographic component of a larger multipsychological service unit or of a governmental, educational, correctional, health, training, industrial, or commercial organizational unit.[6]

C. One or more clinical psychologists providing professional services in a multidisciplinary setting constitute a clinical psychological service unit.

D. A clinical psychological service unit may also be one or more clinical psychologists in a private practice or a psychological consulting firm.

Users of clinical psychological services include:

A. Direct users or recipients of clinical psychological services.

B. Public and private institutions, facilities, or organizations receiving clinical psychological services.

C. Third-party purchasers—those who pay for the delivery of services but who are not the recipients of services.

D. Sanctioners—those who have a legitimate concern with the accessibility, timeliness, efficacy, and standards of quality attending the provision of clinical psychological services. Sanctioners may include members of the user's family, the court, the probation officer, the school administrator, the employer, the union representative, the facility director, and so on. Sanctioners may also include various governmental, peer review, and accreditation bodies concerned with the assurance of quality.

Guideline 1
PROVIDERS

1.1 *Each clinical psychological service unit offering psychological services has available at least one professional clinical psychologist and as many more professional clinical psychologists as are necessary to assure the adequacy and quality of services offered.*

INTERPRETATION: The intent of this Guideline is that one or more providers of psychological services in any clinical psychological service unit meet the levels of training and experience of the professional clinical psychologist as specified in the preceding definitions.[7]

When a facility offering clinical psychological services does not have a full-time professional clinical psychologist available, the facility retains the services of one or more professional clinical psychologists on a regular part-time basis. The clinical psychologist so retained directs and supervises the psychological services provided, participates sufficiently to be able to assess the need for services, reviews the content of services provided, and has the authority to assume professional responsibility and accountability for them.

The psychologist directing the service unit is responsible for determining and justifying appropriate ratios of psychologists to users and psychologists to support staff, in order to ensure proper scope, accessibility, and quality of services provided in that setting.

1.2 *Providers of clinical psychological services who do not meet the requirements for the professional clinical psychologist are supervised directly by a professional clinical psychologist who assumes professional responsibility and accountability for the services provided. The level and extent of supervision may vary from task to task so long as the supervising psychologist retains a sufficiently close supervisory relationship to meet this Guideline. Special proficiency training or supervision may be provided by a professional psychologist of another specialty or by a professional from another discipline whose competence in the given area has been demonstrated by previous training and experience.*

INTERPRETATION: In each clinical psychological service unit there may be varying levels of responsibility with respect to the nature and quality of services provided. Support personnel are considered to be responsible for their functions and behavior when assisting in the provision of clinical psychological services and are accountable to the professional clinical psychologist. Ultimate professional responsibility and accountability for the services provided require that the supervisor review and approve reports and test protocols, review and approve intervention plans and strategies, and review outcomes. Therefore, the supervision of all clinical psychological services is provided directly by a professional clinical

psychologist in individual and/or group face-to-face meetings.

In order to meet this Guideline, an appropriate number of hours per week are devoted to direct face-to-face supervision of each clinical psychological service unit staff member. In no event is such supervision less than 1 hour per week. The more comprehensive the psychological services are, the more supervision is needed. A plan or formula for relating increasing amounts of supervisory time to the complexity of professional responsibilities is to be developed. The amount and nature of supervision is made known to all parties concerned.

Such communications are in writing and describe and delineate the duties of the employee with respect to range and type of services to be provided. The limits of independent action and decision making are defined. The description of responsibility also specifies the means by which the employee will contact the professional clinical psychologist in the event of emergency or crisis situations.

1.3 *Wherever a clinical psychological service unit exists, a professional clinical psychologist is responsible for planning, directing, and reviewing the provision of clinical psychological services. Whenever the clinical psychological service unit is part of a larger professional psychological service encompassing various psychological specialties, a professional psychologist is the administrative head of the service.*

INTERPRETATION: The clinical psychologist coordinates the activities of the clinical psychological service unit with other professional, administrative, and technical groups, both within and outside the facility. This clinical psychologist, who may be the director, chief, or coordinator of the clinical psychological service unit, has related responsibilities including, but not limited to, recruiting qualified staff, directing training and research activities of the service, maintaining a high level of professional and ethical practice, and ensuring that staff members function only within the areas of their competency.

To facilitate the effectiveness of clinical services by raising the level of staff sensitivity and professional skills, the clinical psychologist designated as director is responsible for participating in the selection of staff and support personnel whose qualifications and skills (e.g., language, cultural and experiential background, race, sex, and age) are directly relevant to the needs and characteristics of the users served.

1.4 *When functioning as part of an organizational setting, professional clinical psychologists bring their backgrounds and skills to bear on the goals of the organization, whenever appropriate, by participation in the planning and development of overall services.*[8]

INTERPRETATION: Professional clinical psychologists participate in the maintenance of high professional standards by representation on committees concerned with service delivery.

As appropriate to the setting, their activities may include active participation, as voting and as office-holding members, on the professional staffs of hospitals and other facilities and on other executive, planning, and evaluation boards and committees.

1.5 *Clinical psychologists maintain current knowledge of scientific and professional developments to preserve and enhance their professional competence.*[9]

INTERPRETATION: Methods through which knowledge of scientific and professional developments may be gained include, but are not limited to, reading scientific and professional publications, attendance at workshops, participation in staff development programs, and other forms of continuing education. The clinical psychologist has ready access to reference material related to the provision of psychological services. Clinical psychologists are prepared to show evidence periodically that they are staying abreast of current knowledge and practices in the field of clinical psychology through continuing education.

1.6 *Clinical psychologists limit their practice to their demonstrated areas of professional competence.*

INTERPRETATION: Clinical psychological services are offered in accordance with the providers' areas of competence as defined by verifiable training and experience. When extending services beyond the range of their usual practice, psychologists obtain pertinent training or appropriate professional supervision. Such training or supervision is consistent with the extension of functions performed and services provided. An extension of services may involve a change in the theoretical orientation of the clinical psychologist, a change in modality or technique, or a change in the type of client and/or the kinds of problems or disorders for which services are to be provided (e.g., children, elderly persons, mental retardation, neurological impairment).

1.7 *Professional psychologists who wish to qualify as clinical psychologists meet the same requirements with respect to subject matter and professional skills that apply to doctoral and postdoctoral education and training in clinical psychology.*[10]

INTERPRETATION: Education of doctoral-level psychologists to qualify them for specialty practice in clinical psychology is under the auspices of a department in a regionally accredited university or of a professional school that offers the doctoral degree in clinical psychology. Such education is individualized, with due credit being given for relevant course work and other requirements that have previously been satisfied. In addition, doctoral-level training plus 1 year of postdoctoral experience supervised by a clinical psychologist is re-

quired. Merely taking an internship in clinical psychology or acquiring experience in a practicum setting is not adequate preparation for becoming a clinical psychologist when prior education has not been in that area. Fulfillment of such an individualized educational program is attested to by the awarding of a certificate by the supervising department or professional school that indicates the successful completion of preparation in clinical psychology.

1.8 *Professional clinical psychologists are encouraged to develop innovative theories and procedures and to provide appropriate theoretical and/or empirical support for their innovations.*

INTERPRETATION: A specialty of a profession rooted in a science intends continually to explore and experiment with a view to developing and verifying new and improved methods of serving the public in ways that can be documented.

Guideline 2
PROGRAMS

2.1 *Composition and organization of a clinical psychological service unit:*

2.1.1 *The composition and programs of a clinical psychological service unit are responsive to the needs of the persons or settings served.*

INTERPRETATION: A clinical psychological service unit is structured so as to facilitate effective and economical delivery of services. For example, a clinical psychological service unit serving predominantly a low-income, ethnic, or racial minority group has a staffing pattern and service programs that are adapted to the linguistic, experiential, and attitudinal characteristics of the users.

2.1.2 *A description of the organization of the clinical psychological service unit and its lines of responsibility and accountability for the delivery of psychological services is available in written form to staff of the unit and to users and sanctioners upon request.*

INTERPRETATION: The description includes lines of responsibility, supervisory relationships, and the level and extent of accountability for each person who provides psychological services.

2.1.3 *A clinical psychological service unit includes sufficient numbers of professional and support personnel to achieve its goals, objectives, and purposes.*

INTERPRETATION: The work load and diversity of psychological services required and the specific goals and objectives of the setting determine the numbers and qualifications of professional and support personnel in the clinical psychological service unit. Where shortages in personnel exist, so that psychological services cannot be rendered in a professional manner, the director of the clinical psychological service unit initiates action to remedy such shortages. When this fails, the director appropriately modifies the scope or work load of the unit to maintain the quality of the services rendered.

2.2 Policies:

2.2.1 *When the clinical psychological service unit is composed of more than one person or is a component of a larger organization, a written statement of its objectives and scope of services is developed, maintained, and reviewed.*

INTERPRETATION: The clinical psychological service unit reviews its objectives and scope of services annually and revises them as necessary to ensure that the psychological services offered are consistent with staff competencies and current psychological knowledge and practice. This statement is discussed with staff, reviewed with the appropriate administrator, and distributed to users and sanctioners upon request, whenever appropriate.

2.2.2 *All providers within a clinical psychological service unit support the legal and civil rights of the users.*[11]

INTERPRETATION: Providers of clinical psychological services safeguard the interests of the users with regard to personal, legal, and civil rights. They are continually sensitive to the issue of confidentiality of information, the short-term and long-term impacts of their decisions and recommendations, and other matters pertaining to individual, legal, and civil rights. Concerns regarding the safeguarding of individual rights of users include, but are not limited to, problems of self-incrimination in judicial proceedings, involuntary commitment to hospitals, protection of minors or legal incompetents, discriminatory practices in employment selection procedures, recommendation for special education provisions, information relative to adverse personnel actions in the armed services, and adjudication of domestic relations disputes in divorce and custodial proceedings. Providers of clinical psychological services take affirmative action by making themselves available to local committees, review boards, and similar advisory groups established to safeguard the human, civil, and legal rights of service users.

2.2.3 *All providers within a clinical psychological service unit are familiar with and adhere to the American Psychological Association's* Standards for Providers of Psychological Services, Ethical Principles of Psychologists, Standards for Educational and Psychological Tests, Ethical Principles in the Conduct of Research With Human Participants, *and other official policy statements relevant to standards for professional services issued by the Association.*

INTERPRETATION: Providers of clinical psychological services maintain up-to-date knowledge of the relevant standards of the American Psychological Association.

2.2.4 *All providers within a clinical psychological service unit conform to relevant statutes established by federal, state, and local governments.*

INTERPRETATION: All providers of clinical psychological services are familiar with appropriate statutes regulating the practice of psychology. They observe agency regulations that have the force of law and that relate to the delivery of psychological services (e.g., evaluation for disability retirement and special education placements). In addition, all providers are cognizant that federal agencies such as the Veterans Administration, the Department of Education, and the Department of Health and Human Services have policy statements regarding psychological services, and where relevant, providers conform to them. Providers of clinical psychological services are also familiar with other statutes and regulations, including those addressed to the civil and legal rights of users (e.g., those promulgated by the federal Equal Employment Opportunity Commission), that are pertinent to their scope of practice.

It is the responsibility of the American Psychological Association to maintain current files of those federal policies, statutes, and regulations relating to this section and to assist its members in obtaining them. The state psychological associations and the state licensing boards periodically publish and distribute appropriate state statutes and regulations.

2.2.5 *All providers within a clinical psychological service unit inform themselves about and use the network of human services in their communities in order to link users with relevant services and resources.*

INTERPRETATION: Clinical psychologists and support staff are sensitive to the broader context of human needs. In recognizing the matrix of personal and societal problems, providers make available to users information regarding human services such as legal aid societies, social services, employment agencies, health resources, and educational and recreational facilities. Providers of clinical psychological services refer to such community resources and, when indicated, actively intervene on behalf of the users.

Community resources include the private as well as the public sectors. Private resources include private agencies and centers and psychologists in independent private practice. Consultation is sought or referral made within the public or private network of services whenever required in the best interest of the users. Clinical psychologists, in either the private or the public setting, utilize other resources in the community whenever indicated because of limitations within the psychological service unit providing the services. Professional clinical psychologists in private practice are familiar with the types of services offered through local community mental health clinics and centers, including alternatives to hospitalization, and know the costs and eligibility requirements for those services.

2.2.6 *In the delivery of clinical psychological services, the providers maintain a cooperative relationship with colleagues and co-workers in the best interest of the users.*[12]

INTERPRETATION: Clinical psychologists recognize the areas of special competence of other professional psychologists and of professionals in other fields for either consultation or referral purposes. Providers of clinical psychological services make appropriate use of other professional, research, technical, and administrative resources to serve the best interests of users and establish and maintain cooperative arrangements with such other resources as required to meet the needs of users.

2.3 Procedures:

2.3.1 *Each clinical psychological service unit follows a set of procedural guidelines for the delivery of psychological services.*

INTERPRETATION: Providers are prepared to provide a statement of procedural guidelines, in either oral or written form, in terms that can be understood by users, including sanctioners and local administrators. This statement describes the current methods, forms, procedures, and techniques being used to achieve the objectives and goals for psychological services.

2.3.2 *Providers of clinical psychological services develop plans appropriate to the providers' professional practices and to the problems presented by the users.*

INTERPRETATION: A clinical psychologist develops a plan that describes the psychological services, their objectives, and the manner in which they will be provided.[13,14] This plan is in written form; it serves as a basis for obtaining understanding and concurrence from the user and provides a mechanism for subsequent peer review. This plan is, of course, modified as new needs or information develops.

A clinical psychologist who provides services as one member of a collaborative effort participates in the development and implementation of the overall service plan and provides for its periodic review.

2.3.3 *Accurate, current, and pertinent documentation of essential clinical psychological services provided is maintained.*

INTERPRETATION: Records kept of clinical psychological services may include, but are not limited to, identifying data, dates of services, types of services, significant actions taken, and outcome at termination. Providers of clinical psychological services ensure that essential information concerning services rendered is recorded within a reasonable time following their completion.

2.3.4 *Each clinical psychological service unit follows an established record retention and disposition policy.*

INTERPRETATION: The policy on record retention and disposition conforms to federal or state statutes or administrative regulations where such are applicable. In the absence of such regulations, the policy is (a) that the full record be retained intact for 3 years after the completion of planned services or after the date of last contact with the user, whichever is later; (b) that a full record or summary of the record be maintained for an additional 12 years; and (c) that the record may be disposed of no sooner than 15 years after the completion of planned services or after the date of the last contact, whichever is later. These temporal guides are consistent with procedures currently in use by federal record centers.

In the event of the death or incapacity of a clinical psychologist in independent practice, special procedures are necessary to ensure the continuity of active services to users and the proper safeguarding of inactive records being retained to meet this Guideline. Following approval by the affected user, it is appropriate for another clinical psychologist, acting under the auspices of the local professional standards review committee (PSRC), to review the records with the user and recommend a course of action for continuing professional service, if needed. Depending on local circumstances, the reviewing psychologist may also recommend appropriate arrangements for the balance of the record retention and disposition period.

This Guideline has been designed to meet a variety of circumstances that may arise, often years after a set of psychological services has been completed. More and more records are being used in forensic matters, for peer review, and in response to requests from users, other professionals, or other legitimate parties requiring accurate information about the exact dates, nature, course, and outcome of a set of psychological services. These record retention procedures also provide valuable baseline data for the original psychologist–provider when a previous user returns for additional services.

2.3.5 *Providers of clinical psychological services maintain a system to protect confidentiality of their records.*[15]

INTERPRETATION: Clinical psychologists are responsible for maintaining the confidentiality of information about users of services, from whatever source derived. All persons supervised by clinical psychologists, including nonprofessional personnel and students, who have access to records of psychological services are required to maintain this confidentiality as a condition of employment.

The clinical psychologist does not release confidential information, except with the written consent of the user directly involved or his or her legal representative. Even after consent for release has been obtained, the clinical psychologist clearly identifies such information as confidential to the recipient of the information.[16] If directed otherwise by statute or regulations with the force of law or by court order, the psychologist may seek a resolution to the conflict that is both ethically and legally feasible and appropriate.

Users are informed in advance of any limits in the setting for maintenance of confidentiality of psychological information. For instance, clinical psychologists in hospital, clinic, or agency settings inform their patients that psychological information in a patient's clinical record may be available without the patient's written consent to other members of the professional staff associated with the patient's treatment or rehabilitation. Similar limitations on confidentiality of psychological information may be present in certain school, industrial, military, or other institutional settings, or in instances in which the user has waived confidentiality for purposes of third-party payment.

Users have the right to obtain information from their psychological records. However, the records are the property of the psychologist or the facility in which the psychologist works and are, therefore, the responsibility of the psychologist and subject to his or her control.

When the user's intention to waive confidentiality is judged by the professional clinical psychologist to be contrary to the user's best interests or to be in conflict with the user's civil and legal rights, it is the responsibility of the clinical psychologist to discuss the implications of releasing psychological information and to assist the user in limiting disclosure only to information required by the present circumstance.

Raw psychological data (e.g., questionnaire returns or test protocols) in which a user is identified are released only with the written consent of the user or his or her legal representative and released only to a person recognized by the clinical psychologist as qualified and competent to use the data.

Any use made of psychological reports, records, or data for research or training purposes is consistent with this Guideline. Additionally, providers of clinical psychological services comply with statutory confidentiality requirements and those embodied in the American Psychological Association's *Ethical Principles of Psychologists* (APA, 1981b).

Providers of clinical psychological services remain sensitive to both the benefits and the possible misuse of information regarding individuals that is stored in large computerized data banks. Providers use their influence to ensure that such information is used in a socially responsible manner.

Guideline 3
ACCOUNTABILITY

3.1 *The clinical psychologist's professional activity is guided primarily by the principle of promoting human welfare.*

INTERPRETATION: Clinical psychologists provide services to users in a manner that is considerate, effective, economical, and humane. Clinical psychologists make their services readily accessible to users in a manner that facilitates the users' freedom of choice.

Clinical psychologists are mindful of their accountability to the sanctioners of clinical psychological services and to the general public, provided that appropriate steps are taken to protect the confidentiality of the service relationship. In the pursuit of their professional activities, they aid in the conservation of human, material, and financial resources.

The clinical psychological service unit does not withhold services to a potential client on the basis of that user's race, color, religion, gender, sexual orientation, age, or national origin. Recognition is given, however, to the following considerations: the professional right of clinical psychologists to limit their practice to a specific category of users (e.g., children, adolescents, women); the right and responsibility of clinical psychologists to withhold an assessment procedure when not validly applicable; and the right and responsibility of clinical psychologists to withhold evaluative, psychotherapeutic, counseling, or other services in specific instances in which their own limitations or client characteristics might impair the effectiveness of the relationship.[17,18] Clinical psychologists seek to ameliorate through peer review, consultation, or other personal therapeutic procedures those factors that inhibit the provision of services to particular users. When indicated services are not available, clinical psychologists take whatever action is appropriate to inform responsible persons and agencies of the lack of such services.

Clinical psychologists who find that psychological services are being provided in a manner that is discriminatory or exploitative to users and/or contrary to these Guidelines or to state or federal statutes take appropriate corrective action, which may include the refusal to provide services. When conflicts of interest arise, the clinical psychologist is guided in the resolution of differences by the principles set forth in the American Psychological Association's *Ethical Principles of Psychologists* (APA, 1981b) and "Guidelines for Conditions of Employment of Psychologists" (APA, 1972).

3.2 *Clinical psychologists pursue their activities as members of the independent, autonomous profession of psychology.*[19]

INTERPRETATION: Clinical psychologists, as members of an independent profession, are responsible both to the public and to their peers through established review mechanisms. Clinical psychologists are aware of the implications of their activities for the profession as a whole. They seek to eliminate discriminatory practices instituted for self-serving purposes that are not in the interest of the users (e.g., arbitrary requirements for referral and supervision by another profession). They are cognizant of their responsibilities for the development of the profession. They participate where possible in the training and career development of students and other providers, participate as appropriate in the training of paraprofessionals or other professionals, and integrate and supervise the implementation of their contributions within the structure established for delivering psychological services. Clinical psychologists facilitate the development of, and participate in, professional standards review mechanisms.[20]

Clinical psychologists seek to work with other professionals in a cooperative manner for the good of the users and the benefit of the general public. Clinical psychologists associated with multidisciplinary settings support the principle that members of each participating profession have equal rights and opportunities to share all privileges and responsibilities of full membership in hospital facilities or other human service facilities and to administer service programs in their respective areas of competence.

3.3 *There are periodic, systematic, and effective evaluations of clinical psychological services.*[21]

INTERPRETATION: When the clinical psychological service unit is a component of a larger organization, regular evaluation of progress in achieving goals is provided for in the service delivery plan, including consideration of the effectiveness of clinical psychological services relative to costs in terms of use of time and money and the availability of professional and support personnel.

Evaluation of the clinical psychological service delivery system is conducted internally and, when possible, under independent auspices as well. This evaluation includes an assessment of effectiveness (to determine what the service unit accomplished), efficiency (to determine the total costs of providing the services), continuity (to ensure that the services are appropriately linked to other human services), availability (to determine appropriate levels and distribution of services and personnel), accessibility (to ensure that the services are barrier free to users), and adequacy (to determine whether the services meet the identified needs for such services).

There is a periodic reexamination of review mechanisms to ensure that these attempts at public safeguards are effective and cost efficient and do not place unnecessary encumbrances on the providers or impose unnecessary additional expenses on users or sanctioners for services rendered.

3.4 *Clinical psychologists are accountable for all aspects of the services they provide and are responsive to those concerned with these services.*[22]

INTERPRETATION: In recognizing their responsibilities to users, and where appropriate and consistent with the users' legal rights and privileged communications, clinical psychologists make available information about, and provide opportunity to participate in, decisions concerning such issues as initiation, termination, continuation, modification, and evaluation of clinical psychological services.

Depending on the settings, accurate and full information is made available to prospective individual or organizational users regarding the qualifications of providers, the nature and extent of services offered, and where appropriate, financial and social costs.

Where appropriate, clinical psychologists inform users of their payment policies and their willingness to assist in obtaining reimbursement. Those who accept reimbursement from a third party are acquainted with the appropriate statutes and regulations and assist their users in understanding procedures for submitting claims and limits on confidentiality of claims information, in accordance with pertinent statutes.

Guideline 4
ENVIRONMENT

4.1 *Providers of clinical psychological services promote the development in the service setting of a physical, organizational, and social environment that facilitates optimal human functioning.*

INTERPRETATION: Federal, state, and local requirements for safety, health, and sanitation are observed.

As providers of services, clinical psychologists are concerned with the environment of their service unit, especially as it affects the quality of service, but also as it impinges on human functioning when the service unit is included in a larger context. Physical arrangements and organizational policies and procedures are conducive to the human dignity, self-respect, and optimal functioning of users and to the effective delivery of service. Attention is given to the comfort and the privacy of users. The atmosphere in which clinical psychological services are rendered is appropriate to the service and to the users, whether in an office, clinic, school, industrial organization, or other institutional setting.

FOOTNOTES

[1] The footnotes appended to these Specialty Guidelines represent an attempt to provide a coherent context of other policy statements of the Association regarding professional practice. The Guidelines extend these previous policy statements where necessary to reflect current concerns of the public and the profession.

[2] The following two categories of professional psychologists who met the criteria indicated below on or before the adoption of these Specialty Guidelines on January 31, 1980, are also considered clinical psychologists: Category 1—persons who completed (a) a doctoral degree program primarily psychological in content at a regionally accredited university or professional school and (b) 3 postdoctoral years of appropriate education, training, and experience in providing clinical psychological services as defined herein, including a minimum of 1 year in a clinical setting; Category 2—persons who on or before September 4, 1974, (a) completed a master's degree from a program primarily psychological in content at a regionally accredited

11

university or professional school and (b) held a license or certificate in the state in which they practiced, conferred by a state board of psychological examiners, or the endorsement of the state psychological association through voluntary certification, and who, in addition, prior to January 31, 1980, (c) obtained 5 post-master's years of appropriate education, training, and experience in providing clinical psychological services as defined herein, including a minimum of 2 years in a clinical setting.

After January 31, 1980, professional psychologists who wish to be recognized as professional clinical psychologists are referred to Guideline 1.7.

The definition of the professional clinical psychologist in these Guidelines does not contradict or supersede in any way the broader definition accorded the term *clinical psychologist* in the Federal Employees Health Benefits Program (see *Access to Psychologists and Optometrists Under Federal Health Benefits Program*, U.S. Senate Report No. 93-961, June 25, 1974).

[3] The areas of knowledge and training that are a part of the educational program for all professional psychologists have been presented in two APA documents, *Education and Credentialing in Psychology II* (APA, 1977a) and *Criteria for Accreditation of Doctoral Training Programs and Internships in Professional Psychology* (APA, 1979). There is consistency in the presentation of core areas in the education and training of all professional psychologists. The description of education and training in these Guidelines is based primarily on the document *Education and Credentialing in Psychology II*. It is intended to indicate broad areas of required curriculum, with the expectation that training programs will undoubtedly want to interpret the specific content of these areas in different ways depending on the nature, philosophy, and intent of the programs.

[4] Functions and activities of psychologists relating to the teaching of psychology, the writing or editing of scholarly or scientific manuscripts, and the conduct of scientific research do not fall within the purview of these Guidelines.

[5] The definitions should be compared with the APA (1967) guidelines for state legislation (hereinafter referred to as state guidelines), which define *psychologist* and the *practice of psychology* as follows:

A person represents himself [or herself] to be a psychologist when he [or she] holds himself [or herself] out to the public by any title or description of services incorporating the words "psychology," "psychological," "psychologist," and/or offers to render or renders services as defined below to individuals, groups, organizations, or the public for a fee, monetary or otherwise.

The practice of psychology within the meaning of this act is defined as rendering to individuals, groups, organizations, or the public any psychological service involving the application of principles, methods, and procedures of understanding, predicting, and influencing behavior, such as the principles pertaining to learning, perception, motivation, thinking, emotions and interpersonal relationships; the methods and procedures of interviewing, counseling, and psychotherapy; of constructing, administering, and interpreting tests of mental abilities, aptitudes, interests, attitudes, personality characteristics, emotion, and motivation; and of assessing public opinion.

The application of said principles and methods includes, but is not restricted to: diagnosis, prevention, and amelioration of adjustment problems and emotional and mental disorders of individuals and groups; hypnosis; educational and vocational counseling; personnel selection and management; the evaluation and planning for effective work and learning situations; advertising and market research; and the resolution of interpersonal and social conflicts.

Psychotherapy within the meaning of this act means the use of learning, conditioning methods, and emotional reac-

tions, in a professional relationship, to assist a person or persons to modify feelings, attitudes, and behavior which are intellectually, socially, or emotionally maladjustive or ineffectual.

The practice of psychology shall be as defined above, any existing statute in the state of _____ to the contrary notwithstanding. (APA, 1967, pp. 1098–1099)

[6] The relation of a psychological service unit to a larger facility or institution is also addressed indirectly in the APA (1972) "Guidelines for Conditions of Employment of Psychologists" (hereinafter referred to as CEP Guidelines), which emphasizes the roles, responsibilities, and prerogatives of the psychologist when he or she is employed by or provides services for another agency, institution, or business.

[7] This Guideline replaces earlier recommendations in the 1967 state guidelines concerning exemption of psychologists from licensure. Recommendations 8 and 9 of those guidelines read as follows:

Persons employed as psychologists by accredited academic institutions, governmental agencies, research laboratories, and business corporations should be exempted, provided such employees are performing those duties for which they are employed by such organizations, and within the confines of such organizations.

Persons employed as psychologists by accredited academic institutions, governmental agencies, research laboratories, and business corporations consulting or offering their research findings or providing scientific information to like organizations for a fee should be exempted. (APA, 1967, p. 1100)

On the other hand, the 1967 state guidelines specifically denied exemptions under certain conditions, as noted in Recommendations 10 and 11:

Persons employed as psychologists who offer or provide psychological services to the public for a fee, over and above the salary that they receive for the performance of their regular duties, should not be exempted.

Persons employed as psychologists by organizations that sell psychological services to the public should not be exempted. (APA, 1967, pp. 1100–1101)

The present APA policy, as reflected in this Guideline, establishes a single code of practice for psychologists providing covered services to users in any setting. The present position is that a psychologist providing any covered service meets local statutory requirements for licensure or certification. See the section entitled Principles and Implications of the Specialty Guidelines for an elaboration of this position.

[8] A closely related principle is found in the APA (1972) CEP Guidelines:

It is the policy of APA that psychology as an independent profession is entitled to parity with other health and human service professions in institutional practices and before the law. Psychologists in interdisciplinary settings such as colleges and universities, medical schools, clinics, private practice groups, and other agencies expect parity with other professions in such matters as academic rank, board status, salaries, fringe benefits, fees, participation in administrative decisions, and all other conditions of employment, private contractual arrangements, and status before the law and legal institutions. (APA, 1972, p. 333)

[9] See CEP Guidelines (section entitled Career Development) for a closely related statement:

Psychologists are expected to encourage institutions and agencies which employ them to sponsor or conduct career development programs. The purpose to these programs would be to enable psychologists to engage in study for professional advancement and to keep abreast of developments in their field. (APA, 1972, p. 332)

[10] This Guideline follows closely the statement regarding "Policy on Training for Psychologists Wishing to Change Their Specialty" adopted by the APA Council of Representatives in January 1976. Included therein was the implementing provision that "this policy statement shall be incorporated in the guidelines of the Committee on Accreditation so that appropriate sanctions can be brought to bear on university and internship training programs that violate [it]" (Conger, 1976, p. 424).

[11] See also APA's (1981b) *Ethical Principles of Psychologists*, especially Principles 5 (Confidentiality), 6 (Welfare of the Consumer), and 9 (Research with Human Participants); and see *Ethical Principles in the Conduct of Research With Human Participants* (APA, 1973a). Also, in 1978 Division 17 approved in principle a statement on "Principles for Counseling and Psychotherapy With Women," which was designed to protect the interests of female users of clinical psychological services.

[12] Support for this position is found in *Psychology as a Profession* in the section on relations with other professions:

Professional persons have an obligation to know and take into account the traditions and practices of other professional groups with whom they work and to cooperate fully with members of such groups with whom research, service, and other functions are shared. (APA, 1968, p. 5)

[13] One example of a specific application of this principle is found in Guideline 2 in APA's (1973b) "Guidelines for Psychologists Conducting Growth Groups":

The following information should be made available *in writing* [italics added] to all prospective participants:

(*a*) An explicit statement of the purpose of the group;

(*b*) Types of techniques that may be employed;

(*c*) The education, training, and experience of the leader or leaders;

(*d*) The fee and any additional expense that may be incurred;

(*e*) A statement as to whether or not a follow-up service is included in the fee;

(*f*) Goals of the group experience and techniques to be used;

(*g*) Amounts and kinds of responsibility to be assumed by the leader and by the participants. For example, (*i*) the degree to which a participant is free not to follow suggestions and prescriptions of the group leader and other group members; (*ii*) any restrictions on a participant's freedom to leave the group at any time; and

(*h*) Issues of confidentiality. (p. 933)

[14] See APA's (1981a) *APA/CHAMPUS Outpatient Psychological Provider Manual*.

[15] See Principle 5 (Confidentiality) in *Ethical Principles of Psychologists* (APA, 1981b).

[16] Support for the principle of privileged communication is found in at least two policy statements of the Association:

In the interest of both the public and the client and in accordance with the requirements of good professional practice, the profession of psychology seeks recognition of the privileged nature of confidential communications with clients, preferably through statutory enactment or by administrative policy where more appropriate. (APA, 1968, p. 8)

Wherever possible, a clause protecting the privileged nature of the psychologist–client relationship be included.

When appropriate, psychologists assist in obtaining general "across the board" legislation for such privileged communications. (APA, 1967, p. 1103)

[17] This paragraph is directly adapted from the CEP Guidelines (APA, 1972, p. 333).

[18] The CEP Guidelines also include the following:

It is recognized that under certain circumstances, the interests and goals of a particular community or segment of interest in the population may be in conflict with the general welfare. Under such circumstances, the psychologist's professional activity must be primarily guided by the principle of "promoting human welfare." (APA, 1972, p. 334)

[19] Support for the principle of the independence of psychology as a profession is found in the following:

As a member of an autonomous profession, a psychologist rejects limitations upon his [or her] freedom of thought and action other than those imposed by his [or her] moral, legal, and social responsibilities. The Association is always prepared to provide appropriate assistance to any responsible member who becomes subjected to unreasonable limitations upon his [or her] opportunity to function as a practitioner, teacher, researcher, administrator, or consultant. The Association is always prepared to cooperate with any responsible professional organization in opposing any unreasonable limitations on the professional functions of the members of that organization.

This insistence upon professional autonomy has been upheld over the years by the affirmative actions of the courts and other public and private bodies in support of the right of the psychologist—and other professionals—to pursue those functions for which he [or she] is trained and qualified to perform. (APA, 1968, p. 9)

Organized psychology has the responsibility to define and develop its own profession, consistent with the general canons of science and with the public welfare.

Psychologists recognize that other professions and other groups will, from time to time, seek to define the roles and responsibilities of psychologists. The APA opposes such developments on the same principle that it is opposed to the psychological profession taking positions which would define the work and scope of responsibility of other duly recognized professions. (APA, 1972, p. 333)

[20] APA support for peer review is detailed in the following excerpt from the APA (1971) statement entitled "Psychology and National Health Care":

All professions participating in a national health plan should be directed to establish review mechanisms (or performance evaluations) that include not only peer review but active participation by persons representing the consumer. In situations where there are fiscal agents, they should also have representation when appropriate. (p. 1026)

[21] This Guideline on program evaluation is based directly on the following excerpts from two APA position papers:

The quality and availability of health services should be evaluated continuously by both consumers and health professionals. Research into the efficiency and effectiveness of the system should be conducted both internally and under independent auspices. (APA, 1971, p. 1025)

The comprehensive community mental health center should devote an explicit portion of its budget to program evaluation. All centers should inculcate in their staff attention to and respect for research findings; the larger centers have an obligation to set a high priority on basic research and to give formal recognition to research as a legitimate part of the duties of staff members.

. . . Only through explicit appraisal of program effects can worthy approaches be retained and refined, ineffective ones dropped. Evaluative monitoring of program achievements may vary, of course, from the relatively informal to the systematic and quantitative, depending on the importance of the issue, the availablity of resources, and the willingness of those responsible to take risks of substituting informed judgment for evidence. (Smith & Hobbs, 1966, pp. 21–22)

[22] See also the CEP Guidelines for the following statement: "A psychologist recognizes that . . . he [or she] alone is accountable for the consequences and effects of his [or her] services, whether as teacher, researcher, or practitioner. This responsibility cannot be shared, delegated, or reduced" (APA, 1972, p. 334).

REFERENCES

American Psychological Association, Committee on Legislation. A model for state legislation affecting the practice of psychology. *American Psychologist*, 1967, *22*, 1095–1103.

American Psychological Association. *Psychology as a profession*. Washington, D.C.: Author, 1968.

American Psychological Association. Psychology and national health care. *American Psychologist*, 1971, *26*, 1025–1026.

American Psychological Association. Guidelines for conditions of employment of psychologists. *American Psychologist*, 1972, *27*, 331–334.

American Psychological Association. *Ethical principles in the conduct of research with human participants*. Washington, D.C.: Author, 1973. (a)

American Psychological Association. Guidelines for psychologists conducting growth groups. *American Psychologist*, 1973, *28*, 933. (b)

American Psychological Association. *Standards for educational and psychological tests*. Washington, D.C.: Author, 1974. (a)

American Psychological Association. *Standards for providers of psychological services*. Washington, D.C.: Author, 1974. (b)

American Psychological Association. *Education and credentialing in psychology II*. Report of a meeting, June 4–5, 1977. Washington, D.C.: Author, 1977. (a)

American Psychological Association. *Standards for providers of psychological services* (Rev. ed.). Washington, D.C.: Author, 1977. (b)

American Psychological Association. *Criteria for accreditation of doctoral training programs and internships in professional psychology*. Washington, D.C.: Author, 1979 (amended 1980).

American Psychological Association. *APA/CHAMPUS outpatient psychological provider manual* (Rev. ed.). Washington, D.C.: Author, 1981 (a)

American Psychological Association. *Ethical principles of psychologists* (Rev. ed.). Washington, D.C.: Author, 1981. (b)

Conger, J. J. Proceedings of the American Psychological Association, Incorporated, for the year 1975: Minutes of the annual meeting of the Council of Representatives. *American Psychologist*, 1976, *31*, 406–434.

Smith, M. B., & Hobbs, N. *The community and the community mental health center*. Washington, D.C.: American Psychological Association, 1966.

Specialty Guidelines for the Delivery of Services by Counseling Psychologists

The Specialty Guidelines that follow are based on the generic *Standards for Providers of Psychological Services* originally adopted by the American Psychological Association (APA) in September 1974 and revised in January 1977 (APA, 1974b, 1977b). Together with the generic *Standards*, these Specialty Guidelines state the official policy of the Association regarding delivery of services by counseling psychologists. Admission to the practice of psychology is regulated by state statute. It is the position of the Association that licensing be based on generic, and not on specialty, qualifications. Specialty guidelines serve the additional purpose of providing potential users and other interested groups with essential information about particular services available from the several specialties in professional psychology.

Professional psychology specialties have evolved from generic practice in psychology and are supported by university training programs. There are now at least four recognized professional specialties—clinical, counseling, school, and industrial/organizational psychology.

The knowledge base in each of these specialty areas has increased, refining the state of the art to the point that a set of uniform specialty guidelines is now possible and desirable. The present Guidelines are intended to educate the public, the profession, and other interested parties regarding specialty professional practices. They are also intended to facilitate the continued systematic development of the profession.

The content of each Specialty Guideline reflects a consensus of university faculty and public and private practitioners regarding the knowledge base, services provided, problems addressed, and clients served.

Traditionally, all learned disciplines have treated the designation of specialty practice as a reflection of preparation in greater depth in a particular subject matter, together with a voluntary limiting of focus to a more restricted area of practice by the professional. Lack of specialty designation does not preclude general providers of psychological services from using the methods or dealing with the populations of any specialty, except insofar as psychologists voluntarily refrain from providing services they are not trained to render. It is the intent of these guidelines, however, that after the grandparenting period, psychologists not put themselves forward as *specialists* in a given area of practice unless they meet the qualifications noted in the Guidelines (see Definitions). Therefore, these Guidelines are meant to apply only to those psychologists who voluntarily wish to be designated as *counseling psychologists*. They do not apply to other psychologists.

These Guidelines represent the profession's best judgment of the conditions, credentials, and experience that contribute to competent professional practice. The APA strongly encourages, and plans to participate in, efforts to identify professional practitioner behaviors and job functions and to validate the relation between these and desired client outcomes. Thus, future revisions of these Guidelines will increasingly reflect the results of such efforts.

These Guidelines follow the format and, wherever applicable, the wording of the generic *Standards*.[1] (Note: Footnotes appear at the end of the Specialty Guidelines. See pp. 661–663.) The intent of these Guidelines is to improve the quality, effectiveness, and accessibility of psychological services. They are meant to provide guidance to providers, users, and sanctioners regarding the best judgment of the profession on these matters. Although the Specialty Guidelines have been derived from and are consistent with the generic *Standards*, they may be used as separate documents. However, *Standards for Providers of Psychological Services* (APA, 1977b) shall remain the basic policy statement and shall take precedence where there are questions of interpretation.

Professional psychology in general and counseling psychology as a specialty have labored long and diligently to codify a uniform set of guidelines for the delivery of services by counseling psychologists that would serve the respective needs of users, providers, third-party purchasers, and sanctioners of psychological services.

The Committee on Professional Standards, established by the APA in January 1980, is charged with keeping the generic *Standards* and the Specialty Guidelines responsive to the needs of the public and the profession. It is also charged with continually reviewing, modifying, and extending them progressively as the profession and the science of psychology develop new knowledge, improved methods, and additional modes of psychological services.

The Specialty Guidelines for the Delivery of Services by Counseling Psychologists that follow have been established by the APA as a means of self-regulation to protect the public interest. They guide the specialty prac-

These Specialty Guidelines were prepared by the APA Committee on Standards for Providers of Psychological Services (COSPOPS), chaired by Durand F. Jacobs, with the advice of the officers and committee chairpersons of the Division of Counseling Psychology (Division 17). Barbara A. Kirk and Milton Schwebel served successively as the counseling psychology representative of COSPOPS, and Arthur Centor and Richard Kilburg were the Central Office liaisons to the committee. Norman Kagan, Samuel H. Osipow, Carl E. Thoresen, and Allen E. Ivey served successively as Division 17 presidents.

tice of counseling psychology by specifying important areas of quality assurance and performance that contribute to the goal of facilitating more effective human functioning.

Principles and Implications of the Specialty Guidelines

These Specialty Guidelines emerged from and reaffirm the same basic principles that guided the development of the generic *Standards for Providers of Psychological Services* (APA, 1977b):

1. These Guidelines recognize that admission to the practice of psychology is regulated by state statute.

2. It is the intention of the APA that the generic *Standards* provide appropriate guidelines for statutory licensing of psychologists. In addition, although it is the position of the APA that licensing be generic and not in specialty areas, these Specialty Guidelines in counseling psychology provide an authoritative reference for use in credentialing specialty providers of counseling psychological services by such groups as divisions of the APA and state associations and by boards and agencies that find such criteria useful for quality assurance.

3. A uniform set of Specialty Guidelines governs the quality of services to all users of counseling psychological services in both the private and the public sectors. Those receiving counseling psychological services are protected by the same kinds of safeguards, irrespective of sector; these include constitutional guarantees, statutory regulation, peer review, consultation, record review, and supervision.

4. A uniform set of Specialty Guidelines governs counseling psychological service functions offered by counseling psychologists, regardless of setting or form of remuneration. All counseling psychologists in professional practice recognize and are responsive to a uniform set of Specialty Guidelines, just as they are guided by a common code of ethics.

5. Counseling psychology Guidelines establish clear, minimally acceptable levels of quality for covered counseling psychological service functions, regardless of the nature of the users, purchasers, or sanctioners of such covered services.

6. All persons providing counseling psychological services meet specified levels of training and experience that are consistent with, and appropriate to, the functions they perform. Counseling psychological services provided by persons who do not meet the APA qualifications for a professional counseling psychologist (see Definitions) are supervised by a professional counseling psychologist. Final responsibility and accountability for services provided rest with professional counseling psychologists.

7. When providing any of the covered counseling psychological service functions at any time and in any setting, whether public or private, profit or nonprofit, counseling psychologists observe these Guidelines in order to promote the best interests and welfare of the users

of such services. The extent to which counseling psychologists observe these Guidelines is judged by peers.

8. These Guidelines, while assuring the user of the counseling psychologist's accountability for the nature and quality of services specified in this document, do not preclude the counseling psychologist from using new methods or developing innovative procedures in the delivery of counseling services.

These Specialty Guidelines have broad implications both for users of counseling psychological services and for providers of such services:

1. Guidelines for counseling psychological services provide a foundation for mutual understanding between provider and user and facilitate more effective evaluation of services provided and outcomes achieved.

2. Guidelines for counseling psychologists are essential for uniformity in specialty credentialing of counseling psychologists.

3. Guidelines give specific content to the profession's concept of ethical practice as it applies to the functions of counseling psychologists.

4. Guidelines for counseling psychological services may have significant impact on tomorrow's education and training models for both professional and support personnel in counseling psychology.

5. Guidelines for the provision of counseling psychological services in human service facilities influence the determination of acceptable structure, budgeting, and staffing patterns in these facilities.

6. Guidelines for counseling psychological services require continual review and revision.

The Specialty Guidelines here presented are intended to improve the quality and delivery of counseling psychological services by specifying criteria for key aspects of the practice setting. Some settings may require additional and/or more stringent criteria for specific areas of service delivery.

Systematically applied, these Guidelines serve to establish a more effective and consistent basis for evaluating the performance of individual service providers as well as to guide the organization of counseling psychological service units in human service settings.

Definitions

Providers of counseling psychological services refers to two categories of persons who provide counseling psychological services:

A. Professional counseling psychologists.[2] Professional counseling psychologists have a doctoral degree from a regionally accredited university or professional school providing an organized, sequential counseling psychology program in an appropriate academic department in a university or college, or in an appropriate department or unit of a professional school. Counseling psychology programs that are accredited by the American Psychological Association are recognized as meeting the definition of a counseling psychology program. Counseling psychology programs that are not accredited by the American Psychological Association meet the definition of a counseling psychology program if they satisfy the following criteria:

1. The program is primarily psychological in nature and stands as a recognizable, coherent organizational entity within the institution.

2. The program provides an integrated, organized sequence of study.

3. The program has an identifiable body of students who are matriculated in that program for a degree.

4. There is a clear authority with primary responsibility for the core and specialty areas, whether or not the program cuts across administrative lines.

5. There is an identifiable psychology faculty, and a psychologist is responsible for the program.

The professional counseling psychologist's doctoral education and training experience[3] is defined by the institution offering the program. Only counseling psychologists, that is, those who meet the appropriate education and training requirements, have the minimum professional qualifications to provide unsupervised counseling psychological services. A professional counseling psychologist and others providing counseling psychological services under supervision (described below) form an integral part of a multilevel counseling psychological service delivery system.

B. All other persons who provide counseling psychological services under the supervision of a professional counseling psychologist. Although there may be variations in the titles of such persons, they are not referred to as counseling psychologists. Their functions may be indicated by use of the adjective *psychological* preceding the noun, for example, *psychological associate, psychological assistant, psychological technician,* or *psychological aide.*

Counseling psychological services refers to services provided by counseling psychologists that apply principles, methods, and procedures for facilitating effective functioning during the life-span developmental process.[4,5] In providing such services, counseling psychologists approach practice with a significant emphasis on positive aspects of growth and adjustment and with a developmental orientation. These services are intended to help persons acquire or alter personal–social skills, improve adaptability to changing life demands, enhance environmental coping skills, and develop a variety of problem-solving and decision-making capabilities. Counseling psychological services are used by individuals, couples, and families of all age groups to cope with problems connected with education, career choice, work, sex, marriage, family, other social relations, health, aging, and handicaps of a social or physical nature. The services are offered in such organizations as educational, rehabilitation, and health institutions and in a variety of other public and private agencies committed to service in one or more of the problem areas cited above. Counseling psychological services include the following:

A. Assessment, evaluation, and diagnosis. Procedures may include, but are not limited to, behavioral observation, interviewing, and administering and interpreting instruments for the assessment of educational achievement, academic skills, aptitudes, interests, cognitive abilities, attitudes, emotions, motivations, psychoneurological status, personality characteristics, or any other aspect of human experience and behavior that may contribute to understanding and helping the user.

B. Interventions with individuals and groups. Procedures include individual and group psychological counseling (e.g., education, career, couples, and family counseling) and may use a therapeutic, group process, or social-learning approach, or any other deemed to be appropriate. Interventions are used for purposes of prevention, remediation, and rehabilitation; they may incorporate a variety of psychological modalities, such as psychotherapy, behavior therapy, marital and family therapy, biofeedback techniques, and environmental design.

C. Professional consultation relating to A and B above, for example, in connection with developing in-service training for staff or assisting an educational institution or organization to design a plan to cope with persistent problems of its students.

D. Program development services in the areas of A, B, and C above, such as assisting a rehabilitation center to design a career-counseling program.

E. Supervision of all counseling psychological services, such as the review of assessment and intervention activities of staff.

F. Evaluation of all services noted in A through E above and research for the purpose of their improvement.

A *counseling psychological service unit* is the functional unit through which counseling psychological services are provided; such a unit may be part of a larger psychological service organization comprising psychologists of more than one specialty and headed by a professional psychologist:

A. A counseling psychological service unit provides predominantly counseling psychological services and is composed of one or more professional counseling psychologists and supporting staff.

B. A counseling psychological service unit may operate as a functional or geographic component of a larger multipsychological service unit or of a governmental, educational, correctional, health, training, industrial, or commercial organizational unit, or it may operate as an independent professional service.[6]

C. A counseling psychological service unit may take the form of one or more counseling psychologists providing professional services in a multidisciplinary setting.

D. A counseling psychological service unit may also take the form of a private practice, composed of one or more counseling psychologists serving individuals or groups, or the form of a psychological consulting firm serving organizations and institutions.

Users of counseling psychological services include:

A. Direct users or recipients of counseling psychological services.

B. Public and private institutions, facilities, or organizations receiving counseling psychological services.

C. Third-party purchasers—those who pay for the delivery of services but who are not the recipients of services.

D. Sanctioners—those who have a legitimate concern with the accessibility, timeliness, efficacy, and standards of quality attending the provision of counseling psychological services. Sanctioners may include members of the user's family, the court, the probation officer, the school administrator, the employer, the union representative, the facility director, and so on. Sanctioners may also include various governmental, peer review, and accreditation bodies concerned with the assurance of quality.

Guideline 1
PROVIDERS

1.1 *Each counseling psychological service unit offering psychological services has available at least one professional counseling psychologist and as many more professional counseling psychologists as are necessary to assure the adequacy and quality of services offered.*

INTERPRETATION: The intent of this Guideline is that one or more providers of psychological services in any counseling psychological service unit meet the levels of training and experience of the professional counseling psychologist as specified in the preceding definitions.[7]

When a professional counseling psychologist is not available on a full-time basis, the facility retains the services of one or more professional counseling psychologists on a regular part-time basis. The counseling psychologist so retained directs the psychological services, including supervision of the support staff, has the authority and participates sufficiently to assess the need for services, reviews the content of services provided, and assumes professional responsibility and accountability for them.

The psychologist directing the service unit is responsible for determining and justifying appropriate ratios of psychologists to users and psychologists to support staff, in order to ensure proper scope, accessibility, and quality of services provided in that setting.

1.2 *Providers of counseling psychological services who do not meet the requirements for the professional counseling psychologist are supervised directly by a professional counseling psychologist who assumes professional responsibility and accountability for the services provided. The level and extent of supervision may vary from task to task so long as the supervising psychologist retains a sufficiently close supervisory relationship to meet this Guideline. Special proficiency training or supervision may be provided by a professional psycholo-*

gist of another specialty or by a professional from another discipline whose competence in the given area has been demonstrated by previous training and experience.

INTERPRETATION: In each counseling psychological service unit there may be varying levels of responsibility with respect to the nature and quality of services provided. Support personnel are considered to be responsible for their functions and behavior when assisting in the provision of counseling psychological services and are accountable to the professional counseling psychologist. Ultimate professional responsibility and accountability for the services provided require that the supervisor review reports and test protocols, and review and discuss intervention plans, strategies, and outcomes. Therefore, the supervision of all counseling psychological services is provided directly by a professional counseling psychologist in a face-to-face arrangement involving individual and/or group supervision. The extent of supervision is determined by the needs of the providers, but in no event is it less than 1 hour per week for each support staff member providing counseling psychological services.

To facilitate the effectiveness of the psychological service unit, the nature of the supervisory relationship is communicated to support personnel in writing. Such communications delineate the duties of the employees, describing the range and type of services to be provided. The limits of independent action and decision making are defined. The description of responsibility specifies the means by which the employee will contact the professional counseling psychologist in the event of emergency or crisis situations.

1.3 *Wherever a counseling psychological service unit exists, a professional counseling psychologist is responsible for planning, directing, and reviewing the provision of counseling psychological services. Whenever the counseling psychological service unit is part of a larger professional psychological service encompassing various psychological specialties, a professional psychologist shall be the administrative head of the service.*

INTERPRETATION: The counseling psychologist who directs or coordinates the unit is expected to maintain an ongoing or periodic review of the adequacy of services and to formulate plans in accordance with the results of such evaluation. He or she coordinates the activities of the counseling psychology unit with other professional, administrative, and technical groups, both within and outside the institution or agency. The counseling psychologist has related responsibilities including, but not limited to, directing the training and research activities of the service, maintaining a high level of professional and ethical practice, and ensuring that staff members function only within the areas of their competency.

To facilitate the effectiveness of counseling services by raising the level of staff sensitivity and professional skills, the counseling psychologist designated as director is responsible for participating in the selection of staff and support personnel whose qualifications and skills (e.g., language, cultural and experiential background, race, sex, and age) are relevant to the needs and characteristics of the users served.

1.4 *When functioning as part of an organizational setting, professional counseling psychologists bring their backgrounds and skills to bear on the goals of the organization, whenever appropriate, by participation in the planning and development of overall services.*[8]

INTERPRETATION: Professional counseling psychologists participate in the maintenance of high professional standards by representation on committees concerned with service delivery.

As appropriate to the setting, their activities may include active participation, as voting and as office-holding members, on the facility's professional staff and on other executive, planning, and evaluation boards and committees.

1.5 *Counseling psychologists maintain current knowledge of scientific and professional developments to preserve and enhance their professional competence.*

INTERPRETATION: Methods through which knowledge of scientific and professional developments may be gained include, but are not limited to, reading scientific and professional publications, attendance at professional workshops and meetings, participation in staff development programs, and other forms of continuing education.[9] The counseling psychologist has ready access to reference material related to the provision of psychological services. Counseling psychologists are prepared to show evidence periodically that they are staying abreast of current knowledge and practices in the field of counseling psychology through continuing education.

1.6 *Counseling psychologists limit their practice to their demonstrated areas of professional competence.*

INTERPRETATION: Counseling psychological services are offered in accordance with the providers' areas of competence as defined by verifiable training and experience. When extending services beyond the range of their usual practice, counseling psychologists obtain pertinent training or appropriate professional supervision. Such training or supervision is consistent with the extension of functions performed and services provided. An extension of services may involve a change in the theoretical orientation of the counseling psychologist, in the modality or techniques used, in the type of client, or in the kinds of problems or disorders for which services are to be provided.

1.7 *Professional psychologists who wish to qualify as counseling psychologists meet the same requirements*

with respect to subject matter and professional skills that apply to doctoral education and training in counseling psychology.[10]

INTERPRETATION: Education of doctoral-level psychologists to qualify them for specialty practice in counseling psychology is under the auspices of a department in a regionally accredited university or of a professional school that offers the doctoral degree in counseling psychology. Such education is individualized, with due credit being given for relevant course work and other requirements that have previously been satisfied. In addition, doctoral-level training supervised by a counseling psychologist is required. Merely taking an internship in counseling psychology or acquiring experience in a practicum setting is not adequate preparation for becoming a counseling psychologist when prior education has not been in that area. Fulfillment of such an individualized educational program is attested to by the awarding of a certificate by the supervising department or professional school that indicates the successful completion of preparation in counseling psychology.

1.8 *Professional counseling psychologists are encouraged to develop innovative theories and procedures and to provide appropriate theoretical and/or empirical support for their innovations.*

INTERPRETATION: A specialty of a profession rooted in a science intends continually to explore and experiment with a view to developing and verifying new and improved ways of serving the public and documents the innovations.

Guideline 2
PROGRAMS

2.1 *Composition and organization of a counseling psychological service unit:*

2.1.1 *The composition and programs of a counseling psychological service unit are responsive to the needs of the persons or settings served.*

INTERPRETATION: A counseling psychological service unit is structured so as to facilitate effective and economical delivery of services. For example, a counseling psychological service unit serving predominantly a low-income, ethnic, or racial minority group has a staffing pattern and service programs that are adapted to the linguistic, experiential, and attitudinal characteristics of the users.

2.1.2 *A description of the organization of the counseling psychological service unit and its lines of responsibility and accountability for the delivery of psychological services is available in written form to* *staff of the unit and to users and sanctioners upon request.*

INTERPRETATION: The description includes lines of responsibility, supervisory relationships, and the level and extent of accountability for each person who provides psychological services.

2.1.3 *A counseling psychological service unit includes sufficient numbers of professional and support personnel to achieve its goals, objectives, and purposes.*

INTERPRETATION: The work load and diversity of psychological services required and the specific goals and objectives of the setting determine the numbers and qualifications of professional and support personnel in the counseling psychological service unit. Where shortages in personnel exist, so that psychological services cannot be rendered in a professional manner, the director of the counseling psychological service unit initiates action to remedy such shortages. When this fails, the director appropriately modifies the scope or work load of the unit to maintain the quality of the services rendered and, at the same time, makes continued efforts to devise alternative systems for delivery of services.

2.2 *Policies:*

2.2.1 *When the counseling psychological service unit is composed of more than one person or is a component of a larger organization, a written statement of its objectives and scope of services is developed, maintained, and reviewed.*

INTERPRETATION: The counseling psychological service unit reviews its objectives and scope of services annually and revises them as necessary to ensure that the psychological services offered are consistent with staff competencies and current psychological knowledge and practice. This statement is discussed with staff, reviewed with the appropriate administrator, and distributed to users and sanctioners upon request, whenever appropriate.

2.2.2 *All providers within a counseling psychological service unit support the legal and civil rights of the users.*[11]

INTERPRETATION: Providers of counseling psychological services safeguard the interests of the users with regard to personal, legal, and civil rights. They are continually sensitive to the issue of confidentiality of information, the short-term and long-term impacts of their decisions and recommendations, and other matters pertaining to individual, legal, and civil rights. Concerns regarding the safeguarding of individual rights of users include, but are not limited to, problems of access to professional records in educational institutions, self-incrimination in judicial proceedings, involuntary commitment to hos-

pitals, protection of minors or legal incompetents, discriminatory practices in employment selection procedures, recommendation for special education provisions, information relative to adverse personnel actions in the armed services, and adjudication of domestic relations disputes in divorce and custodial proceedings. Providers of counseling psychological services take affirmative action by making themselves available to local committees, review boards, and similar advisory groups established to safeguard the human, civil, and legal rights of service users.

2.2.3 *All providers within a counseling psychological service unit are familiar with and adhere to the American Psychological Association's* Standards for Providers of Psychological Services, Ethical Principles of Psychologists, Standards for Educational and Psychological Tests, Ethical Principles in the Conduct of Research With Human Participants, *and other official policy statements relevant to standards for professional services issued by the Association.*

INTERPRETATION: Providers of counseling psychological services maintain current knowledge of relevant standards of the American Psychological Association.

2.2.4 *All providers within a counseling psychological service unit conform to relevant statutes established by federal, state, and local governments.*

INTERPRETATION: All providers of counseling psychological services are familiar with and conform to appropriate statutes regulating the practice of psychology. They also observe agency regulations that have the force of law and that relate to the delivery of psychological services (e.g., evaluation for disability retirement and special education placements). In addition, all providers are cognizant that federal agencies such as the Veterans Administration, the Department of Education, and the Department of Health and Human Services have policy statements regarding psychological services. Providers are familiar as well with other statutes and regulations, including those addressed to the civil and legal rights of users (e.g., those promulgated by the federal Equal Employment Opportunity Commission), that are pertinent to their scope of practice.

It is the responsibility of the American Psychological Association to maintain current files of those federal policies, statutes, and regulations relating to this section and to assist its members in obtaining them. The state psychological associations and the state licensing boards periodically publish and distribute appropriate state statutes and regulations, and these are on file in the counseling psychological service unit or the larger multipsychological service unit of which it is a part.

2.2.5 *All providers within a counseling psychological service unit inform themselves about and use the* *network of human services in their communities in order to link users with relevant services and resources.*

INTERPRETATION: Counseling psychologists and support staff are sensitive to the broader context of human needs. In recognizing the matrix of personal and social problems, providers make available to clients information regarding human services such as legal aid societies, social services, employment agencies, health resources, and educational and recreational facilities. Providers of counseling psychological services refer to such community resources and, when indicated, actively intervene on behalf of the users.

Community resources include the private as well as the public sectors. Consultation is sought or referral made within the public or private network of services whenever required in the best interest of the users. Counseling psychologists, in either the private or the public setting, utilize other resources in the community whenever indicated because of limitations within the psychological service unit providing the services. Professional counseling psychologists in private practice know the types of services offered through local community mental health clinics and centers, through family-service, career, and placement agencies, and through reading and other educational improvement centers and know the costs and the eligibility requirements for those services.

2.2.6 *In the delivery of counseling psychological services, the providers maintain a cooperative relationship with colleagues and co-workers in the best interest of the users.*[12]

INTERPRETATION: Counseling psychologists recognize the areas of special competence of other professional psychologists and of professionals in other fields for either consultation or referral purposes. Providers of counseling psychological services make appropriate use of other professional, research, technical, and administrative resources to serve the best interests of users and establish and maintain cooperative arrangements with such other resources as required to meet the needs of users.

2.3 *Procedures:*

2.3.1 *Each counseling psychological service unit is guided by a set of procedural guidelines for the delivery of psychological services.*

INTERPRETATION: Providers are prepared to provide a statement of procedural guidelines, in either oral or written form, in terms that can be understood by users, including sanctioners and local administrators. This statement describes the current methods, forms, procedures, and techniques being used to achieve the objectives and goals for psychological services.

2.3.2 *Providers of counseling psychological services develop plans appropriate to the providers' profes-*

sional practices and to the problems presented by the users.

INTERPRETATION: A counseling psychologist, after initial assessment, develops a plan describing the objectives of the psychological services and the manner in which they will be provided.[13] To illustrate, the agreement spells out the objective (e.g., a career decision), the method (e.g., short-term counseling), the roles (e.g., active participation by the user as well as the provider), and the cost. This plan is in written form. It serves as a basis for obtaining understanding and concurrence from the user and for establishing accountability and provides a mechanism for subsequent peer review. This plan is, of course, modified as changing needs dictate.

A counseling psychologist who provides services as one member of a collaborative effort participates in the development, modification (if needed), and implementation of the overall service plan and provides for its periodic review.

2.3.3 *Accurate, current, and pertinent documentation of essential counseling psychological services provided is maintained.*

INTERPRETATION: Records kept of counseling psychological services include, but are not limited to, identifying data, dates of services, types of services, significant actions taken, and outcome at termination. Providers of counseling psychological services ensure that essential information concerning services rendered is recorded within a reasonable time following their completion.

2.3.4 *Each counseling psychological service unit follows an established record retention and disposition policy.*

INTERPRETATION: The policy on record retention and disposition conforms to state statutes or federal regulations where such are applicable. In the absence of such regulations, the policy is (a) that the full record be maintained intact for at least 4 years after the completion of planned services or after the date of last contact with the user, whichever is later; (b) that if a full record is not retained, a summary of the record be maintained for an additional 3 years; and (c) that the record may be disposed of no sooner than 7 years after the completion of planned services or after the date of last contact, whichever is later.

In the event of the death or incapacity of a counseling psychologist in independent practice, special procedures are necessary to ensure the continuity of active service to users and the proper safeguarding of records in accordance with this Guideline. Following approval by the affected user, it is appropriate for another counseling psychologist, acting under the auspices of the professional standards review committee (PSRC) of the state, to review the record with the user and recommend a course of action for continuing professional service, if needed. Depending on local circumstances, appropriate arrangements for record retention and disposition may also be recommended by the reviewing psychologist.

This Guideline has been designed to meet a variety of circumstances that may arise, often years after a set of psychological services has been completed. Increasingly, psychological records are being used in forensic matters, for peer review, and in response to requests from users, other professionals, and other legitimate parties requiring accurate information about the exact dates, nature, course, and outcome of a set of psychological services. The 4-year period for retention of the full record covers the period of either undergraduate or graduate study of most students in postsecondary educational institutions, and the 7-year period for retention of at least a summary of the record covers the period during which a previous user is most likely to return for counseling psychological services in an educational institution or other organization or agency.

2.3.5 *Providers of counseling psychological services maintain a system to protect confidentiality of their records.*[14]

INTERPRETATION: Counseling psychologists are responsible for maintaining the confidentiality of information about users of services, from whatever source derived. All persons supervised by counseling psychologists, including nonprofessional personnel and students, who have access to records of psychological services maintain this confidentiality as a condition of employment and/or supervision.

The counseling psychologist does not release confidential information, except with the written consent of the user directly involved or his or her legal representative. The only deviation from this rule is in the event of clear and imminent danger to, or involving, the user. Even after consent for release has been obtained, the counseling psychologist clearly identifies such information as confidential to the recipient of the information.[15] If directed otherwise by statute or regulations with the force of law or by court order, the psychologist seeks a resolution to the conflict that is both ethically and legally feasible and appropriate.

Users are informed in advance of any limits in the setting for maintenance of confidentiality of psychological information. For instance, counseling psychologists in agency, clinic, or hospital settings inform their clients that psychological information in a client's record may be available without the client's written consent to other members of the professional staff associated with service to the client. Similar limitations on confidentiality of psychological information may be present in certain educational, industrial, military, or other institutional settings, or in instances in which the user has waived confidentiality for purposes of third-party payment.

Users have the right to obtain information from their psychological records. However, the records are the property of the psychologist or the facility in which the psychologist works and are, therefore, the responsibility of the psychologist and subject to his or her control.

When the user's intention to waive confidentiality is judged by the professional counseling psychologist to be contrary to the user's best interests or to be in conflict with the user's civil and legal rights, it is the responsibility of the counseling psychologist to discuss the implications of releasing psychological information and to assist the user in limiting disclosure only to information required by the present circumstance.

Raw psychological data (e.g., questionnaire returns or test protocols) in which a user is identified are released only with the written consent of the user or his or her legal representative and released only to a person recognized by the counseling psychologist as qualified and competent to use the data.

Any use made of psychological reports, records, or data for research or training purposes is consistent with this Guideline. Additionally, providers of counseling psychological services comply with statutory confidentiality requirements and those embodied in the American Psychological Association's *Ethical Principles of Psychologists* (APA, 1981b).

Providers of counseling psychological services who use information about individuals that is stored in large computerized data banks are aware of the possible misuse of such data as well as the benefits and take necessary measures to ensure that such information is used in a socially responsible manner.

Guideline 3
ACCOUNTABILITY

3.1 *The promotion of human welfare is the primary principle guiding the professional activity of the counseling psychologist and the counseling psychological service unit.*

INTERPRETATION: Counseling psychologists provide services to users in a manner that is considerate, effective, economical, and humane. Counseling psychologists are responsible for making their services readily accessible to users in a manner that facilitates the users' freedom of choice.

Counseling psychologists are mindful of their accountability to the sanctioners of counseling psychological services and to the general public, provided that appropriate steps are taken to protect the confidentiality of the service relationship. In the pursuit of their professional activities, they aid in the conservation of human, material, and financial resources.

The counseling psychological service unit does not withhold services to a potential client on the basis of that user's race, color, religion, gender, sexual orientation, age, or national origin; nor does it provide services in a discriminatory or exploitative fashion. Counseling psychologists who find that psychological services are being provided in a manner that is discriminatory or exploitative to users and/or contrary to these Guidelines or to state or federal statutes take appropriate corrective action, which may include the refusal to provide services. When conflicts of interest arise, the counseling psychologist is guided in the resolution of differences by the principles set forth in the American Psychological Association's *Ethical Principles of Psychologists* (APA, 1981b) and "Guidelines for Conditions of Employment of Psychologists" (APA, 1972).[16]

Recognition is given to the following considerations in regard to the withholding of service: (a) the professional right of counseling psychologists to limit their practice to a specific category of users with whom they have achieved demonstrated competence (e.g., adolescents or families); (b) the right and responsibility of counseling psychologists to withhold an assessment procedure when not validly applicable; (c) the right and responsibility of counseling psychologists to withhold services in specific instances in which their own limitations or client characteristics might impair the quality of the services; (d) the obligation of counseling psychologists to seek to ameliorate through peer review, consultation, or other personal therapeutic procedures those factors that inhibit the provision of services to particular individuals; and (e) the obligation of counseling psychologists who withhold services to assist clients in obtaining services from other sources.[17]

3.2 *Counseling psychologists pursue their activities as members of the independent, autonomous profession of psychology.*[18]

INTERPRETATION: Counseling psychologists, as members of an independent profession, are responsible both to the public and to their peers through established review mechanisms. Counseling psychologists are aware of the implications of their activities for the profession as a whole. They seek to eliminate discriminatory practices instituted for self-serving purposes that are not in the interest of the users (e.g., arbitrary requirements for referral and supervision by another profession). They are cognizant of their responsibilities for the development of the profession, participate where possible in the training and career development of students and other providers, participate as appropriate in the training of paraprofessionals or other professionals, and integrate and supervise the implementation of their contributions within the structure established for delivering psychological services. Counseling psychologists facilitate the development of, and participate in, professional standards review mechanisms.[19]

Counseling psychologists seek to work with other professionals in a cooperative manner for the good of the users and the benefit of the general public. Counseling psychologists associated with multidisciplinary settings support the principle that members of each participating profession have equal rights and opportunities to share all privileges and responsibilities of full membership in human service facilities and to administer service programs in their respective areas of competence.

3.3 *There are periodic, systematic, and effective evaluations of counseling psychological services.*[20]

INTERPRETATION: When the counseling psychological service unit is a component of a larger organization, regular evaluation of progress in achieving goals is provided for in the service delivery plan, including consideration of the effectiveness of counseling psychological services relative to costs in terms of use of time and money and the availability of professional and support personnel.

Evaluation of the counseling psychological service delivery system is conducted internally and, when possible, under independent auspices as well. This evaluation includes an assessment of effectiveness (to determine what the service unit accomplished), efficiency (to determine the total costs of providing the services), continuity (to ensure that the services are appropriately linked to other human services), availability (to determine appropriate levels and distribution of services and personnel), accessibility (to ensure that the services are barrier free to users), and adequacy (to determine whether the services meet the identified needs for such services).

There is a periodic reexamination of review mechanisms to ensure that these attempts at public safeguards are effective and cost efficient and do not place unnecessary encumbrances on the providers or impose unnecessary additional expenses on users or sanctioners for services rendered.

3.4 *Counseling psychologists are accountable for all aspects of the services they provide and are responsive to those concerned with these services.*[21]

INTERPRETATION: In recognizing their responsibilities to users, sanctioners, third-party purchasers, and other providers, and where appropriate and consistent with the users' legal rights and privileged communications, counseling psychologists make available information about, and provide opportunity to participate in, decisions concerning such issues as initiation, termination, continuation, modification, and evaluation of counseling psychological services.

Depending on the settings, accurate and full information is made available to prospective individual or organizational users regarding the qualifications of providers, the nature and extent of services offered, and where appropriate, financial and social costs.

Where appropriate, counseling psychologists inform users of their payment policies and their willingness to assist in obtaining reimbursement. To assist their users, those who accept reimbursement from a third party are acquainted with the appropriate statutes and regulations, the procedures for submitting claims, and the limits on confidentiality of claims information, in accordance with pertinent statutes.

Guideline 4
ENVIRONMENT

4.1 *Providers of counseling psychological services promote the development in the service setting of a physical, organizational, and social environment that facilitates optimal human functioning.*

INTERPRETATION: Federal, state, and local requirements for safety, health, and sanitation are observed.

As providers of services, counseling psychologists are concerned with the environment of their service unit, especially as it affects the quality of service, but also as it impinges on human functioning in the larger context. Physical arrangements and organizational policies and procedures are conducive to the human dignity, self-respect, and optimal functioning of users and to the effective delivery of service. Attention is given to the comfort and the privacy of providers and users. The atmosphere in which counseling psychological services are rendered is appropriate to the service and to the users, whether in an office, clinic, school, college, university, hospital, industrial organization, or other institutional setting.

FOOTNOTES

[1] The footnotes appended to these Specialty Guidelines represent an attempt to provide a coherent context of other policy statements of the Association regarding professional practice. The Guidelines extend these previous policy statements where necessary to reflect current concerns of the public and the profession.

[2] The following two categories of professional psychologists who met the criteria indicated below on or before the adoption of these Specialty Guidelines on January 31, 1980, are also considered counseling psychologists: Category 1—persons who completed (a) a doctoral degree program primarily psychological in content at a regionally accredited university or professional school and (b) 3 postdoctoral years of appropriate education, training, and experience in providing counseling psychological services as defined herein, including a minimum of 1 year in a counseling setting; Category 2—persons who on or before September 4, 1974, (a) completed a master's degree from a program primarily psychological in content at a regionally accredited university or professional school and (b) held a license or certificate in the state in which they practiced, conferred by a state board of psychological examiners, or the endorsement of the state psychological association through voluntary certification, and who, in addition, prior to January 31, 1980, (c) obtained 5 post-master's years of appropriate education, training, and experience in providing counseling psychological services as defined herein, including a minimum of 2 years in a counseling setting.

After January 31, 1980, professional psychologists who wish to be recognized as professional counseling psychologists are referred to Guideline 1.7.

[3] The areas of knowledge and training that are a part of the educational program for all professional psychologists have been presented in two APA documents, *Education and Credentialing in Psychology II* (APA, 1977a) and *Criteria for Accreditation of Doctoral Training Programs and Internships in Professional Psychology* (APA, 1979). There is consistency in the presentation of core areas in the education and training of all professional psychologists. The description of education and training in these Guidelines is based primarily on the document *Education and Credentialing in Psychology II*. It is intended to indicate broad areas of required curriculum, with the expectation that training programs will undoubtedly want to interpret the specific content of these areas in different ways depending on the nature, philosophy, and intent of the programs.

[4] Functions and activities of counseling psychologists relating to the teaching of psychology, the writing or editing of scholarly or scientific manuscripts, and the conduct of scientific research do not fall within the purview of these Guidelines.

[5] These definitions should be compared with the APA (1967) guidelines for state legislation (hereinafter referred to as state guidelines), which define *psychologist* (i.e., the generic professional psychologist, not the specialist counseling psychologist) and the *practice of psychology* as follows:

A person represents himself [or herself] to be a psychologist when he [or she] holds himself [or herself] out to the public by any title or description of services incorporating the words "psychology," "psychological," "psychologist," and/or offers to render or renders services as defined below to individuals, groups, organizations, or the public for a fee, monetary or otherwise.

The practice of psychology within the meaning of this act is defined as rendering to individuals, groups, organizations, or the public any psychological service involving the application of principles, methods, and procedures of understanding, predicting, and influencing behavior, such as the principles pertaining to learning, perception, motivation, thinking, emotions, and interpersonal relationships; the methods and procedures of interviewing, counseling, and psychotherapy; of constructing, administering, and interpreting tests of mental abilities, aptitudes, interests, attitudes, personality characteristics, emotion, and motivation; and of assessing public opinion.

The application of said principles and methods includes, but is not restricted to: diagnosis, prevention, and amelioration of adjustment problems and emotional and mental disorders of individuals and groups; hypnosis; educational and vocational counseling; personnel selection and management; the evaluation and planning for effective work and learning situations; advertising and market research; and the resolution of interpersonal and social conflicts.

Psychotherapy within the meaning of this act means the use of learning, conditioning methods, and emotional reactions, in a professional relationship, to assist a person or persons to modify feelings, attitudes, and behavior which are intellectually, socially, or emotionally maladjustive or ineffectual.

The practice of psychology shall be as defined above, any existing statute in the state of _____ to the contrary notwithstanding. (APA, 1967, pp. 1098–1099)

[6] The relation of a psychological service unit to a larger facility or institution is also addressed indirectly in the APA (1972)

"Guidelines for Conditions of Employment of Psychologists" (hereinafter referred to as CEP Guidelines), which emphasize the roles, responsibilities, and prerogatives of the psychologist when he or she is employed by or provides services for another agency, institution, or business.

[7] This Guideline replaces earlier recommendations in the 1967 state guidelines concerning exemption of psychologists from licensure. Recommendations 8 and 9 of those guidelines read as follows:

Persons employed as psychologists by accredited academic institutions, governmental agencies, research laboratories, and business corporations should be exempted, provided such employees are performing those duties for which they are employed by such organizations, and within the confines of such organizations.

Persons employed as psychologists by accredited academic institutions, governmental agencies, research laboratories, and business corporations consulting or offering their research findings or providing scientific information *to like organizations* for a fee should be exempted. (APA, 1967, p. 1100)

On the other hand, the 1967 state guidelines specifically denied exemptions under certain conditions, as noted in Recommendations 10 and 11:

Persons employed as psychologists who offer or provide psychological services to the public for a fee, over and above the salary that they receive for the performance of their regular duties, should not be exempted.

Persons employed as psychologists by organizations that sell psychological services to the public should not be exempted. (APA, 1967, pp. 1100–1101)

The present APA policy, as reflected in this Guideline, establishes a single code of practice for psychologists providing covered services to users in any setting. The present position is that a psychologist providing any covered service meets local statutory requirements for licensure or certification. See the section entitled Principles and Implications of the Specialty Guidelines for further elaboration of this point.

[8] A closely related principle is found in the APA (1972) CEP Guidelines:

It is the policy of APA that psychology as an independent profession is entitled to parity with other health and human service professions in institutional practices and before the law. Psychologists in interdisciplinary settings such as colleges and universities, medical schools, clinics, private practice groups, and other agencies expect parity with other professions in such matters as academic rank, board status, salaries, fringe benefits, fees, participation in administrative decisions, and all other conditions of employment, private contractual arrangements, and status before the law and legal institutions. (APA, 1972, p. 333)

[9] See CEP Guidelines (section entitled Career Development) for a closely related statement:

Psychologists are expected to encourage institutions and agencies which employ them to sponsor or conduct career development programs. The purpose of these programs would be to enable psychologists to engage in study for professional advancement and to keep abreast of developments in their field. (APA, 1972, p. 332)

[10] This Guideline follows closely the statement regarding "Policy on Training for Psychologists Wishing to Change Their Specialty" adopted by the APA Council of Representatives in January 1976. Included therein was the implementing provision

that "this policy statement shall be incorporated in the guidelines of the Committee on Accreditation so that appropriate sanctions can be brought to bear on university and internship training programs that violate [it]" (Conger, 1976, p. 424).

[11] See also APA's (1981b) *Ethical Principles of Psychologists*, especially Principles 5 (Confidentiality), 6 (Welfare of the Consumer), and 9 (Research With Human Participants); and see *Ethical Principles in the Conduct of Research With Human Participants* (APA, 1973a). Also, in 1978 Division 17 approved in principle a statement on "Principles for Counseling and Psychotherapy With Women," which was designed to protect the interests of female users of counseling psychological services.

[12] Support for this position is found in the section on relations with other professions in *Psychology as a Profession*:

Professional persons have an obligation to know and take into account the traditions and practices of other professional groups with whom they work and to cooperate fully with members of such groups with whom research, service, and other functions are shared. (APA, 1968, p. 5)

[13] One example of a specific application of this principle is found in APA's (1981a) revised *APA/CHAMPUS Outpatient Psychological Provider Manual*. Another example, quoted below, is found in Guideline 2 in APA's (1973b) "Guidelines for Psychologists Conducting Growth Groups":

The following information should be made available *in writing* [italics added] to all prospective participants:
(*a*) An explicit statement of the purpose of the group;
(*b*) Types of techniques that may be employed;
(*c*) The education, training, and experience of the leader or leaders;
(*d*) The fee and any additional expense that may be incurred;
(*e*) A statement as to whether or not a follow-up service is included in the fee;
(*f*) Goals of the group experience and techniques to be used;
(*g*) Amounts and kinds of responsibility to be assumed by the leader and by the participants. For example, (*i*) the degree to which a participant is free not to follow suggestions and prescriptions of the group leader and other group members; (*ii*) any restrictions on a participant's freedom to leave the group at any time; and
(*h*) Issues of confidentiality. (p. 933)

[14] See Principle 5 (Confidentiality) in *Ethical Principles of Psychologists* (APA, 1981b).

[15] Support for the principles of privileged communication is found in at least two policy statements of the Association:

In the interest of both the public and the client and in accordance with the requirements of good professional practice, the profession of psychology seeks recognition of the privileged nature of confidential communications with clients, preferably through statutory enactment or by administrative policy where more appropriate. (APA, 1968, p. 8)

Wherever possible, a clause protecting the privileged nature of the psychologist–client relationship be included.

When appropriate, psychologists assist in obtaining general "across the board" legislation for such privileged communications. (APA, 1967, p. 1103)

[16] The CEP Guidelines include the following;

It is recognized that under certain circumstances, the interests and goals of a particular community or segment of interest in the population may be in conflict with the general welfare. Under such circumstances, the psychologist's professional activity must be primarily guided by the principle of "promoting human welfare." (APA, 1972, p. 334)

[17] This paragraph is adapted in part from the CEP Guidelines (APA, 1972, p. 333).

[18] Support for the principle of the independence of psychology as a profession is found in the following:

As a member of an autonomous profession, a psychologist rejects limitations upon his [or her] freedom of thought and action other than those imposed by his [or her] moral, legal, and social responsibilities. The Association is always prepared to provide appropriate assistance to any responsible member who becomes subjected to unreasonable limitations upon his [or her] opportunity to function as a practitioner, teacher, researcher, administrator, or consultant. The Association is always prepared to cooperate with any responsible professional organization in opposing any unreasonable limitations on the professional functions of the members of that organization.

This insistence upon professional autonomy has been upheld over the years by the affirmative actions of the courts and other public and private bodies in support of the right of the psychologist—and other professionals—to pursue those functions for which he [or she] is trained and qualified to perform. (APA, 1968, p. 9)

Organized psychology has the responsibility to define and develop its own profession, consistent with the general canons of science and with the public welfare.

Psychologists recognize that other professions and other groups will, from time to time, seek to define the roles and responsibilities of psychologists. The APA opposes such developments on the same principle that it is opposed to the psychological profession taking positions which would define the work and scope of responsibility of other duly recognized professions. (APA, 1972, p. 333)

[19] APA support for peer review is detailed in the following excerpt from the APA (1971) statement entitled "Psychology and National Health Care":

All professions participating in a national health plan should be directed to establish review mechanisms (or performance evaluations) that include not only peer review but active participation by persons representing the consumer. In situations where there are fiscal agents, they should also have representation when appropriate. (p. 1026)

[20] This Guideline on program evaluation is based directly on the following excerpts from two APA position papers:

The quality and availability of health services should be evaluated continuously by both consumers and health professionals. Research into the efficiency and effectiveness of the system should be conducted both internally and under independent auspices. (APA, 1971, p. 1025)

The comprehensive community mental health center should devote an explicit portion of its budget to program evaluation. All centers should inculcate in their staff attention to and respect for research findings; the larger centers have an obligation to set a high priority on basic research and to give formal recognition to research as a legitimate part of the duties of staff members.

. . . Only through explicit appraisal of program effects can worthy approaches be retained and refined, ineffective ones dropped. Evaluative monitoring of program achievements may vary, of course, from the relatively informal to the systematic and quantitative, depending on the importance of the issue, the availability of resources, and the willingness of those responsible to take risks of substituting informed judgment for evidence. (Smith & Hobbs, 1966, pp. 21–22)

[21] See also the CEP Guidelines for the following statement: "A psychologist recognizes that . . . he [or she] alone is accountable for the consequences and effects of his [or her] services, whether as teacher, researcher, or practitioner. This responsibility cannot be shared, delegated, or reduced" (APA, 1972, p. 334).

REFERENCES

American Psychological Association, Committee on Legislation. A model for state legislation affecting the practice of psychology. *American Psychologist*, 1967, 22, 1095–1103.

American Psychological Association. *Psychology as a profession*. Washington, D.C.: Author, 1968.

American Psychological Association. Psychology and national health care. *American Psychologist*, 1971, 26, 1025–1026.

American Psychological Association. Guidelines for conditions of employment of psychologists. *American Psychologist*, 1972, 27, 331–334.

American Psychological Association. *Ethical principles in the conduct of research with human participants*. Washington, D.C.: Author, 1973. (a)

American Psychological Association. Guidelines for psychologists conducting growth groups. *American Psychologist*, 1973, 28, 933. (b)

American Psychological Association. *Standards for educational and psychological tests*. Washington, D.C.: Author, 1974. (a)

American Psychological Association. *Standards for providers of psychological services*. Washington, D.C.: Author, 1974. (b)

American Psychological Association. *Education and credentialing in psychology II*. Report of a meeting, June 4–5, 1977. Washington, D.C.: Author, 1977. (a)

American Psychological Association. *Standards for providers of psychological services* (Rev. ed.). Washington, D.C.: Author, 1977. (b)

American Psychological Association. *Criteria for accreditation of doctoral training programs and internships in professional psychology*. Washington, D.C.: Author, 1979 (amended 1980).

American Psychological Association. *APA/CHAMPUS outpatient psychological provider manual* (Rev. ed.). Washington, D.C.: Author, 1981. (a)

American Psychological Association. *Ethical principles of psychologists* (Rev. ed.). Washington, D.C.: Author, 1981. (b)

Conger, J. J. Proceedings of the American Psychological Association, Incorporated, for the year 1975: Minutes of the annual meeting of the Council of Representatives. *American Psychologist*, 1976, 31, 406–434.

Smith, M. B., & Hobbs, N. *The community and the community mental health center*. Washington, D.C.: American Psychological Association, 1966.

Specialty Guidelines
for the Delivery of Services by
Industrial/Organizational Psychologists

The Specialty Guidelines that follow are supplements to the generic *Standards for Providers of Psychological Services*, originally adopted by the American Psychological Association (APA) in September 1974 and revised in January 1977 (APA, 1974b, 1977). Admission to the practice of psychology is regulated by state statute. It is the position of the Association that licensing be based on generic, and not on specialty, qualifications. Specialty guidelines serve the additional purpose of providing potential users and other interested groups with essential information about particular services available from the several specialties in professional psychology. Although the original APA *Standards* were designed to fill the needs of several classes of psychological practitioners and a wide variety of users, the diversity of professional practice and the use of psychological services require specialty guidelines to clarify the special nature of both practitioners and users. These Specialty Guidelines for the Delivery of Services by Industrial/Organizational (I/O) Psychologists are designed to define the roles of I/O psychologists and the particular needs of users of I/O psychological services.

Professional psychology specialties have evolved from generic practice in psychology and are supported by university training programs. There are now at least four recognized professional specialties—clinical, counseling, school, and industrial/organizational psychology.

The knowledge base in each of these specialty areas has increased, refining the state of the art to the point that a set of uniform specialty guidelines is now possible and desirable. The present Guidelines are intended to educate the public, the profession, and other interested parties regarding specialty professional practices. They are also intended to facilitate the continued systematic development of the profession.

The content of each specialty guideline reflects a consensus of university faculty and public and private practitioners regarding the knowledge base, services provided, problems addressed, and clients served.

Traditionally, all learned disciplines have treated the designation of specialty practice as a reflection of preparation in greater depth in a particular subject matter, together with a voluntary limiting of focus to a more restricted area of practice by the professional. Lack of specialty designation does not preclude general providers of psychological services from using the methods or dealing with the populations of any specialty, except insofar as psychologists voluntarily refrain from providing services they are not trained to render. It is the intent of these Guidelines, however, that after the grandparenting period, psychologists not put themselves forward as *specialists* in a given area of practice unless they meet the qualifications noted in the Guidelines (see Definitions). Therefore, these Guidelines are meant to apply only to those psychologists who voluntarily wish to be designated as *industrial/organizational psychologists*. They do not apply to other psychologists.

These Guidelines represent the profession's best judgment of the conditions, credentials, and experience that contribute to competent professional practice. The APA strongly encourages, and plans to participate in, efforts to identify professional practitioner behaviors and job functions and to validate the relation between these and desired client outcomes. Thus, future revisions of these Guidelines will increasingly reflect the results of such efforts.

Like the APA generic *Standards*, the I/O Specialty Guidelines are concerned with improving the quality, effectiveness, and accessibility of psychological services for all who require benefit from them. These Specialty Guidelines are intended to clarify questions of interpretation of the APA generic *Standards* as they are applied to I/O psychology.

This document presents the APA's position on I/O practice. Ethical standards applicable to I/O psychologists are already in effect,[1] as are other documents that provide guidance to I/O practitioners in specific applications of I/O psychology.[2] (Note: Footnotes appear at the end of the Specialty Guidelines. See p. 669.)

The Committee on Professional Standards established by the APA in January 1980 is charged with keeping the generic *Standards* and the Specialty Guidelines responsive to the needs of the public and the profession. It is also charged with continually reviewing, modifying, and

These Specialty Guidelines were prepared through the cooperative efforts of the APA Committee on Standards for Providers of Psychological Services (COSPOPS), chaired by Durand F. Jacobs, and the APA Division of Industrial and Organizational Psychology (Division 14). Virginia Ellen Schein and Frank Friedlander served as the I/O representatives on COSPOPS, and Arthur Centor and Richard Kilburg served as the Central Office liaisons to the committee. Thomas E. Tice and C. J. Bartlett were the key liaison persons from the Division 14 Professional Affairs Committee. Drafts of these Guidelines were reviewed and commented on by members of the Division 14 Executive Committee.

extending them progressively as the profession and the science of psychology develop new knowledge, improved methods, and additional modes of psychological services.

The Specialty Guidelines for the Delivery of Services by Industrial/Organizational Psychologists that follow have been established by the APA as a means of self-regulation to protect the public interest. They guide the specialty practice of I/O psychology by specifying important areas of quality assurance and performance that contribute to the goal of facilitating more effective human functioning.

Principles and Implications of the Specialty Guidelines

These Specialty Guidelines have emerged from and reaffirm the same basic principles that guided the development of the generic *Standards for Providers of Psychological Services* (APA, 1977):

1. These Guidelines recognize that where the practice of I/O psychology is regulated by federal, state, or local statutes, all providers of I/O psychological services conform to such statutes.

2. A uniform set of Specialty Guidelines governs I/O psychological service functions offered by I/O psychologists, regardless of setting or form of remuneration. All I/O psychologists in professional practice recognize and are responsive to a uniform set of Specialty Guidelines, just as they are guided by a common code of ethics.

3. The I/O Specialty Guidelines establish clearly articulated levels of quality for covered I/O psychological service functions, regardless of the nature of the users, purchasers, or sanctioners of such covered services.

4. All persons providing I/O psychological services meet specified levels of training and experience that are consistent with, and appropriate to, the functions they perform. Persons providing such services who do not meet the APA qualifications for a professional I/O psychologist (see Definitions) are supervised by a psychologist with the requisite training. This level of qualification is necessary to ensure that the public receives services of high quality. Final responsibility and accountability for services provided rest with professional I/O psychologists.

5. These Specialty Guidelines for I/O psychologists are intended to present the APA's position on levels for training and professional practice and to provide clarification of the APA generic *Standards*.

6. A uniform set of Specialty Guidelines governs the quality of I/O psychological services in both the private and the public sectors. Those receiving I/O psychological services are protected by the same kinds of safeguards, irrespective of sector.

7. All persons representing themselves as I/O psychologists at any time and in any setting, whether public or private, profit or nonprofit, observe these Guidelines in order to promote the interests and welfare of the users of I/O psychological services. Judgment of the degree to which these Guidelines are observed take into consideration the capabilities for evaluation and the circumstances that prevail in the setting at the time the program or service is evaluated.

8. These Guidelines, while assuring the user of the I/O psychologist's accountability for the nature and quality of services rendered, do not preclude the providers of I/O psychological services from using new methods or developing innovative procedures in the delivery of such services.

These Specialty Guidelines have broad implications both for users of I/O psychological services and for providers of such services:

1. Guidelines for I/O psychological services provide a basis for a mutual understanding between provider and user and facilitate effective evaluation of services provided and outcomes achieved.

2. Guidelines for I/O psychological services make an important contribution toward greater uniformity in legislative and regulatory actions involving I/O psychologists. Guidelines for providers of I/O psychological services may be useful for uniformity in specialty credentialing of I/O psychologists, if such specialty credentialing is required.

3. Although guidelines for I/O psychological services may have an impact on tomorrow's training models for both professional and support personnel in I/O psychology, they are not intended to interfere with innovations in the training of I/O psychologists.

4. Guidelines for I/O psychological services require continual review and revision.

The Specialty Guidelines here presented are intended to improve the quality and delivery of I/O psychological services by specifying criteria for key aspects of the practice setting. Some settings may require additional and/or more stringent criteria for specific areas of service delivery.

Definitions

A fully qualified *I/O psychologist* has a doctoral degree earned in a program primarily psychological in nature. This degree may be from a department of psychology or from a school of business, management, or administrative science in a regionally accredited university. Consistent with the commitment of I/O psychology to the scientist–professional model, I/O psychologists are thoroughly prepared in basic scientific methods as well as in psychological science; therefore, programs that do not include training in basic scientific methods and research are not considered appropriate educational and training models for I/O psychologists. The I/O psychology doctoral program provides training in (a) scientific and professional ethics, (b) general psychological science, (c) research design and methodology, (d) quantitative and qualitative methodology, and (e) psychological measurement, as well as (f) a supervised practicum or laboratory experience in an area of I/O psychology, (g) a field experience in the application and delivery of I/O services, (h) practice in the conduct of applied research, (i) training in other areas of psychology, in business, and in the social and behavioral sciences, as appropriate, and (j) preparation of a doctoral research dissertation.[3]

Although persons who do not meet all of the above qualifications may provide I/O psychological services, such services are performed under the supervision of a fully qualified I/O psychologist. The supervising I/O psychologist may be a full-time member of the same organization or may be retained on a part-time basis. Psychologists so retained have the authority and participate sufficiently to assess the need for services, to review the services provided, and to ensure professional responsibility and accountability for them. Special proficiency training or supervision may be provided by professional psychologists of other specialties or by professionals of other disciplines whose competencies in the given area have been demonstrated by previous training and experience.

Industrial/organizational psychological services involve the development and application of psychological theory and methodology to problems of organizations and problems of individuals and groups in organizational settings. The purpose of such applications to the assessment, development, or evaluation of individuals, groups, or organizations is to enhance the effectiveness of these individuals, groups, or organizations. The following areas represent some examples of such applications:

A. Selection and placement of employees. Services include development of selection programs, optimal placement of key personnel, and early identification of management potential.

B. Organization development. Services include analyzing organizational structure, formulating corporate personnel strategies, maximizing the effectiveness and satisfaction of individuals and work groups, effecting organizational change, and counseling employees for purposes of improving employee relations, personal and career development, and superior–subordinate relations.

C. Training and development of employees. Services include identifying training and development needs; formulating and implementing programs for technical training, management training, and organizational development; and evaluating the effectiveness of training and development programs in relation to productivity and satisfaction criteria.

D. Personnel research. Services include continuing development of assessment tools for selection, placement, classification, and promotion of employees; validating test instruments; and measuring the effect of cultural factors on test performance.

E. Improving employee motivation. Services include enhancing the productive output of employees, identifying and improving factors associated with job satisfaction, and redesigning jobs to make them more meaningful.

F. Design and optimization of work environments. Services include designing work environments and optimizing person–machine effectiveness.

Guideline 1
PROVIDERS

Staffing and Qualifications of Staff

1.1 *Professional I/O psychologists maintain current knowledge of scientific and professional developments that are related to the services they render.*

INTERPRETATION: Methods through which knowledge of scientific and professional development may be gained include, but are not limited to, continuing education, attendance at workshops, participation in staff development, and reading scientific publications.

The I/O psychologist has ready access to reference material related to the provision of psychological services.

1.2 *Professional I/O psychologists limit their practice to their demonstrated areas of professional competence.*

INTERPRETATION: I/O psychological services are offered in accordance with the providers' areas of competence as defined by verifiable training and experience.

When extending services beyond the range of their usual practice, professional I/O psychologists obtain pertinent training or appropriate professional supervision.

1.3 *Professional psychologists who wish to change their specialty to I/O areas meet the same requirements with respect to subject matter and professional skills that apply to doctoral training in the new specialty.*

INTERPRETATION: Education and training of doctoral-level psychologists, when prior preparation has not been in the I/O area, includes education and training in the content, methodology, and practice of I/O psychology. Such preparation is individualized and may be acquired in a number of ways. Formal education in I/O psychology under the auspices of university departments that offer the doctoral degree in I/O psychology, with certification by the supervising department indicating competency in I/O psychology, is recommended. However, continuing education courses and workshops in I/O psychology, combined with supervised experience as an I/O psychologist, may also be acceptable.

1.4 *Professional I/O psychologists are encouraged to develop innovative procedures and theory.*

INTERPRETATION: Although these Guidelines give examples of I/O psychologist activities, such activities are not limited to those provided. I/O psychologists are encouraged to develop innovative ways of approaching problems.

Guideline 2
PROFESSIONAL CONSIDERATIONS

Protecting the User

2.1 *I/O psychological practice supports the legal and civil rights of the user.*

INTERPRETATION: Providers of I/O psychological services safeguard the interests of the user with regard to legal and civil rights. I/O psychologists are especially sensitive to issues of confidentiality of information. In the case of dual users (e.g., individuals and organizations), I/O psychologists, insofar as possible, anticipate possible conflicts of interest and clarify with both users how such conflicts might be resolved. In addition, I/O service providers make every effort to safeguard documents and files containing confidential information.

2.2 *All providers of I/O psychological services abide by policies of the American Psychological Association that are relevant to I/O psychologists.*

INTERPRETATION: While many official APA policies are relevant to I/O psychology, such as those embodied in the *Ethical Principles of Psychologists* (APA, 1981) and the *Standards of Educational and Psychological Tests* (APA, 1974a), it is recognized that some specific policies which apply only to certain subspecialties (e.g., health care providers) may not be applicable to I/O psychologists.

2.3 *All providers within an I/O psychological service unit are familiar with relevant statutes, regulations, and legal precedents established by federal, state, and local governmental groups.*

INTERPRETATION: Insofar as statutes exist relevant to the practice of the I/O psychological service provider, the provider is familiar with them and conforms to the law. In addition, the provider is familiar with statutes that may govern activities of the user as they relate to services provided. For example, an I/O psychologist who establishes selection systems for a user is aware of and conforms to the statutes governing selection systems for that user. This guideline does not imply that inappropriate statutes, regulations, and legal precedents cannot be opposed through legal processes.

Although I/O psychologists may be required by law to be licensed or certified, most I/O psychological services can be provided by persons who are not licensed or certified. Examples of such services are the administration of standardized group tests of mental abilities, aptitudes, personality characteristics, and so on for in-

structional or personnel screening uses; interviews, such as employment or curriculum advisory interviews, that do not involve the assessment of individual personality characteristics; the design, administration, and interpretation of opinion surveys; the design and evaluation of person–machine systems; the conduct of employee development programs; the counseling of employees by supervisors regarding job performance and working relationships; and the teaching of psychological principles or techniques that do not involve ameliorative services to individuals or groups.

Planning Organizational Goals

2.4 *Providers of I/O psychological services state explicitly what can and cannot reasonably be expected from the services.*

INTERPRETATION: In marketing psychological services, the I/O psychologist realistically appraises the chances of meeting the client's goal(s) and informs the client of the degree of success that can be anticipated. Since the user may or may not possess sophistication in psychological methods and applications, the limitations are stated in terms that are comprehensible to the user.

In presenting statements of reasonable anticipation, the I/O psychologist attempts to be accurate in all regards. This guideline also applies to statements of personal competency and of the competency and experience of the psychological service unit that the I/O psychologist represents. Statements and materials do not make claims or suggest benefits that are not supportable by scientifically acceptable evidence. Since the I/O psychologist may stand to gain financially through the recommendation of a given product or service, particular sensitivity to such issues is essential to avoid compromise of professional responsibilities and objectives.

2.5 *Providers of I/O psychological services do not seek to gain competitive advantage through the use of privileged information.*

INTERPRETATION: In the course of work with a user, I/O practitioners may become aware of the management practices, organizational structure, personnel policies, or financial structure of competing units. Since such information is usually revealed in a privileged context, it is not employed for competitive advantage. Similarly, practitioners may be called on to review the proposal of a competing unit. Information so gained is not used to gain competitive advantage.

2.6 *Providers of I/O psychological services who purchase the services of another psychologist provide a clear statement of the role of the purchaser.*

INTERPRETATION: When an I/O psychological service unit purchases the services of another such unit, the purchasing unit states in advance whether it perceives its role as that of a collaborator, a technical advisor, a scientific monitor, or an informed layperson. The purchaser clearly defines its anticipated role, specifies the extent to which it wishes to be involved in various aspects of program planning and work definition, and describes how differences of opinion on technical and scientific matters are to be resolved. Members of the staff of both the unit purchasing services and the unit providing services are made fully aware of the various role definitions. Deferring all major project decisions to the purchaser is not necessarily considered appropriate in scientific development.

2.7 *Providers of I/O psychological services establish a system to protect confidentiality of their records.*

INTERPRETATION: I/O psychologists are responsible for maintaining the confidentiality of information about users of services, whether obtained by themselves or by those they supervise. All persons supervised by I/O psychologists, including nonprofessional personnel and students, who have access to records of psychological services are required to maintain this confidentiality as a condition of employment.

The I/O psychologist does not release confidential information, except with the written consent of the user directly involved or the user's legal representative. Even after the consent for release has been obtained, the I/O psychologist clearly identifies such information as confidential to the recipient of the information. If directed otherwise by statute or regulations with the force of law or by court order, the psychologist seeks a resolution to the conflict that is both ethically and legally feasible and appropriate.

Users are informed in advance of any limits in the setting for maintenance of confidentiality of psychological information.

When the user intends to waive confidentiality, the psychologist discusses the implications of releasing psychological information and assists the user in limiting disclosure only to information required by the present circumstances.

Raw psychological data (e.g., test protocols, interview notes, or questionnaire returns) in which a user is identified are released only with the written consent of the user or the user's legal representative and released only to a person recognized by the I/O psychologist as qualified and competent to use the data. (Note: The user may be an individual receiving career counseling, in which case individual confidentiality must be maintained, or the user may be an organization, in which case individual data may be shared with others within the organization. When individual information is to be shared with others, e.g., managers, the individual supplying the information is made aware of how this information is to be used.)

Any use made of psychological reports, records, or data for research or training purposes is consistent with this Guideline. Additionally, providers of I/O psychological services comply with statutory confidentiality requirements and those embodied in the American Psychological Association's *Ethical Principles of Psychologists* (APA, 1981).

Providers of I/O psychological services remain sensitive to both the benefits and the possible misuse of information regarding individuals that is stored in computerized data banks. Providers use their influence to ensure that such information is used in a socially responsible manner.

Guideline 3
ACCOUNTABILITY

Evaluating I/O Psychological Services

3.1 *The professional activities of providers of I/O psychological services are guided primarily by the principle of promoting human welfare.*

INTERPRETATION: I/O psychologists do not withhold services to a potential client on the basis of race, color, religion, sex, age, handicap, or national origin. Recognition is given, however, to the following considerations: the professional right of I/O psychologists to limit their practice to avoid potential conflict of interest (e.g., as between union and management, plaintiff and defendant, or business competitors); the right and responsibility of psychologists to withhold a procedure when it is not validly applicable; the right and responsibility of I/O psychologists to withhold evaluative, diagnostic, or change procedures or other services where they might be ineffective or detrimental to the achievement of goals and fulfillment of needs of individuals or organizations.

I/O psychologists who find that psychological services are being provided in a manner that is discriminatory or exploitative to users and/or contrary to these Guidelines or to state or federal statutes take appropriate corrective action, which may include the refusal to provide services. When conflicts of interest arise, the I/O psychologist is guided in the resolution of differences by the principles set forth by the American Psychological Association in the *Ethical Principles of Psychologists* (APA, 1981) and the "Guidelines for Conditions of Employment of Psychologists" (APA, 1972).

3.2 *There are periodic, systematic, and effective evaluations of psychological services.*

INTERPRETATION: Regular assessment of progress in achieving goals and meeting needs is provided in all I/O psychological service units. Such assessment includes both the validation of psychological services designed to predict outcomes and the evaluation of psychological services designed to induce organizational or individual change. This evaluation includes consideration of the effectiveness of I/O psychological services relative to costs in terms of use of time and money and the availability of professional and support personnel.

Evaluation of the efficiency and effectiveness of the I/O psychological service delivery system is conducted internally and, when possible, under independent auspices as well.

It is clearly explained to the user that evaluation of services is a necessary part of providing I/O psychological services and that the cost of such evaluation is justified as part of the cost of services.

FOOTNOTES

[1] See *Ethical Principles of Psychologists* (APA, 1981).

[2] See *Principles for the Validation and Use of Personnel Selection Procedures* (APA Division of Industrial and Organizational Psychology, 1980).

[3] The following two categories of persons who met the criteria indicated below on or before the adoption of these Specialty Guidelines on January 31, 1980, shall also be considered professional I/O psychologists: Category 1—persons who on or before September 4, 1974, (a) completed a master's degree from a program primarily psychological in content at a regionally accredited university, (b) completed 5 post-master's years of appropriate education, training, and experience in providing I/O psychological services as defined herein in the Definitions section, including a minimum of 2 years in an organizational setting, and (c) received a license or certificate in the state in which they practiced, conferred by a state board of psychological examiners; Category 2—persons who completed (a) a doctoral degree from a program primarily psychological in content at a regionally accredited university and (b) 3 postdoctoral years of appropriate education, training, and experience in providing I/O services as defined herein in the Definitions section, including a minimum of 1 year in an organizational setting.

REFERENCES

American Psychological Association. Guidelines for conditions of employment of psychologists. *American Psychologist*, 1972, 27, 331–334.

American Psychological Association. *Standards for educational and psychological tests.* Washington, D.C.: Author, 1974. (a)

American Psychological Association. *Standards for providers of psychological services.* Washington, D.C.: Author, 1974. (b)

American Psychological Association. *Standards for providers of psychological services* (Rev. ed.). Washington, D.C.: Author, 1977.

American Psychological Association, Division of Industrial and Organizational Psychology. *Principles for the validation and use of personnel selection procedures* (2nd ed.). Berkeley, Calif.: Author, 1980. (Copies may be ordered from Lewis E. Albright, Kaiser Aluminum & Chemical Corporation, 300 Lakeside Drive—Room KB 2140, Oakland, California 94643.)

American Psychological Association. *Ethical principles of psychologists* (Rev. ed.). Washington, D.C.: Author, 1981.

Specialty Guidelines for the Delivery of Services by School Psychologists

The Specialty Guidelines that follow are based on the generic *Standards for Providers of Psychological Services* originally adopted by the American Psychological Association (APA) in September 1974 and revised in January 1977 (APA, 1974b, 1977b). Together with the generic *Standards*, these Specialty Guidelines state the official policy of the Association regarding delivery of services by school psychologists. Admission to the practice of psychology is regulated by state statute. It is the position of the Association that licensing be based on generic, and not on specialty, qualifications. Specialty guidelines serve the additional purpose of providing potential users and other interested groups with essential information about particular services available from the several specialties in professional psychology.

Professional psychology specialties have evolved from generic practice in psychology and are supported by university training programs. There are now at least four recognized professional specialties—clinical, counseling, school, and industrial/organizational psychology.

The knowledge base in each of these specialty areas has increased, refining the state of the art to the point that a set of uniform specialty guidelines is now possible and desirable. The present Guidelines are intended to educate the public, the profession, and other interested parties regarding specialty professional practices. They are also intended to facilitate the continued systematic development of the profession.

The content of each Specialty Guideline reflects a consensus of university faculty and public and private practitioners regarding the knowledge base, services provided, problems addressed, and clients served.

Traditionally, all learned disciplines have treated the designation of specialty practice as a reflection of preparation in greater depth in a particular subject matter, together with a voluntary limiting of focus to a more restricted area of practice by the professional. Lack of specialty designation does not preclude general providers of psychological services from using the methods or dealing with the populations of any specialty, except insofar as psychologists voluntarily refrain from providing services they are not trained to render. It is the intent of these Guidelines, however, that after the grandparenting period, psychologists not put themselves forward as *specialists* in a given area of practice unless they meet the qualifications noted in the Guidelines (see Definitions). Therefore, these Guidelines are meant to apply only to those psychologists who wish to be designated as *school psychologists*. They do not apply to other psychologists.

These Guidelines represent the profession's best judgment of the conditions, credentials, and experience that contribute to competent professional practice. The APA strongly encourages, and plans to participate in, efforts to identify professional practitioner behaviors and job functions and to validate the relation between these and desired client outcomes. Thus, future revisions of these Guidelines will increasingly reflect the results of such efforts.

These Guidelines follow the format and, wherever applicable, the wording of the generic *Standards*.[1] (Note: Footnotes appear at the end of the Specialty Guidelines. See pp. 679–681.) The intent of these Guidelines is to improve the quality, effectiveness, and accessibility of psychological services. They are meant to provide guidance to providers, users and sanctioners regarding the best judgment of the profession on these matters. Although the Specialty Guidelines have been derived from and are consistent with the generic *Standards*, they may be used as a separate document. *Standards for Providers of Psychological Services* (APA, 1977b), however, shall remain the basic policy statement and shall take precedence where there are questions of interpretation.

Professional psychology in general and school psychology in particular have had a long and difficult history of attempts to establish criteria for determining guidelines for the delivery of services. In school psychology, state departments of education have traditionally had a strong influence on the content of programs required for certification and on minimum competency levels for practice, leading to wide variations in requirements among the many states. These national Guidelines will reduce confusion, clarify important dimensions of specialty practice, and provide a common basis for peer review of school psychologists' performance.

The Committee on Professional Standards established by the APA in January 1980 is charged with keeping the generic *Standards* and the Specialty Guidelines respon-

These Specialty Guidelines were prepared through the cooperative efforts of the APA Committee on Standards for Providers of Psychological Services (COSPOPS) and the APA Professional Affairs Committee of the Division of School Psychology (Division 16). Jack I. Bardon and Nadine M. Lambert served as the school psychology representatives of COSPOPS, and Arthur Centor and Richard Kilburg were the Central Office liaisons to the committee. Durand F. Jacobs served as chair of COSPOPS, and Walter B. Pryzwansky chaired the Division 16 committee. Drafts of the school psychology Guidelines were reviewed and commented on by members of the Executive Committee of Division 16, representatives of the National Association of School Psychologists, state departments of education, consultants in school psychology, and many professional school psychologists in training programs and in practice in the schools.

sive to the needs of the public and the profession. It is also charged with continually reviewing, modifying, and extending them progressively as the profession and the science of psychology develop new knowledge, improved methods, and additional modes of psychological services.

The Specialty Guidelines for the Delivery of Services by School Psychologists have been established by the APA as a means of self-regulation to protect the public interest. They guide the specialty practice of school psychology by specifying important areas of quality assurance and performance that contribute to the goal of facilitating more effective human functioning.

Principles and Implications of the Specialty Guidelines

These Specialty Guidelines have emerged from and reaffirm the same basic principles that guided the development of the generic *Standards for Providers of Psychological Services* (APA, 1977b):

1. These Guidelines recognize that admission to the practice of school psychology is regulated by state statute.

2. It is the intention of the APA that the generic *Standards* provide appropriate guidelines for statutory licensing of psychologists. In addition, although it is the position of the APA that licensing be generic and not in specialty areas, these Specialty Guidelines in school psychology should provide an authoritative reference for use in credentialing specialty providers of school psychological services by such groups as divisions of the APA and state associations and by boards and agencies that find such criteria useful for quality assurance.

3. A uniform set of Specialty Guidelines governs school psychological service functions offered by school psychologists, regardless of setting or source of remuneration. All school psychologists in professional practice recognize and are responsive to a uniform set of Specialty Guidelines, just as they are guided by a common code of ethics.

4. School psychology Guidelines establish clearly articulated levels of training and experience that are consistent with, and appropriate to, the functions performed. School psychological services provided by persons who do not meet the APA qualifications for a professional school psychologist (see Definitions) are to be supervised by a professional school psychologist. Final responsibility and accountability for services provided rest with professional school psychologists.

5. A uniform set of Specialty Guidelines governs the quality of services to all users of school psychological services in both the private and the public sectors. Those receiving school psychological services are protected by the same kinds of safeguards, irrespective of sector; these include constitutional guarantees, statutory regulation, peer review, consultation, record review, and staff supervision.

6. These Guidelines, while assuring the user of the school psychologist's accountability for the nature and quality of services specified in this document, do not preclude the school psychologist from using new methods or developing innovative procedures for the delivery of school psychological services.

These Specialty Guidelines for school psychology have broad implications both for users of school psychological services and for providers of such services:

1. Guidelines for school psychological services provide a foundation for mutual understanding between provider and user and facilitate more effective evaluation of services provided and outcomes achieved.

2. Guidelines for school psychological services are essential for uniformity of regulation by state departments of education and other regulatory or legislative agencies concerned with the provision of school psychological services. In addition, they provide the basis for state approval of training programs and for the development of accreditation procedures for schools and other facilities providing school psychological services.

3. Guidelines give specific content to the profession's concept of ethical practice as it applies to the functions of school psychologists.

4. Guidelines for school psychological services have significant impact on tomorrow's education and training models for both professional and support personnel in school psychology.

5. Guidelines for the provision of school psychological services influence the determination of acceptable structure, budgeting, and staffing patterns in schools and other facilities using these services.

6. Guidelines for school psychological services require continual review and revision.

The Specialty Guidelines presented here are intended to improve the quality and the delivery of school psychological services by specifying criteria for key aspects of the service setting. Some school settings may require additional and/or more stringent criteria for specific areas of service delivery.

Systematically applied, these Guidelines serve to establish a more effective and consistent basis for evaluating the performance of individual service providers as well as to guide the organization of school psychological service units.

Definitions

Providers of school psychological services refers to two categories of persons who provide school psychological services:

A. Professional school psychologists.[2,3] Professional school psychologists have a doctoral degree from a regionally accredited university or professional school providing an organized, sequential school psychology program in a department of psychology in a university or college, in an appropriate department of a school of education or other similar administrative organization, or in a unit of a professional school. School psychology programs that are accredited by the American Psychological Association are recognized as meeting the definition of a school psychology program. School psychology programs that are not accredited by the American Psychological Association meet the definition of a school psychology program if they satisfy the following criteria:

1. The program is primarily psychological in nature and stands as a recognizable, coherent organizational entity within the institution.

2. The program provides an integrated, organized sequence of study.

3. The program has an identifiable body of students who are matriculated in that program for a degree.

4. There is a clear authority with primary responsibility for the core and specialty areas, whether or not the program cuts across administrative lines.

5. There is an identifiable psychology faculty, and a psychologist is responsible for the program.

Patterns of education and training in school psychology[4] are consistent with the functions to be performed and the services to be provided, in accordance with the ages, populations, and problems found in the various schools and other settings in which school psychologists are employed. The program of study includes a core of academic experience, both didactic and experiential, in basic areas of psychology, includes education related to the practice of the specialty, and provides training in assessment, intervention, consultation, research, program development, and supervision, with special emphasis on school-related problems or school settings.[5]

Professional school psychologists who wish to represent themselves as proficient in specific applications of school psychology that are not already part of their training are required to have further academic training and supervised experience in those areas of practice.

B. All other persons who offer school psychological services under the supervision of a school psychologist. Although there may be variations in the titles and job descriptions of such persons, they are not called school psychologists. Their functions may be indicated by use of the adjective *psychological* preceding the noun.

1. A *specialist in school psychology* has successfully completed at least 2 years of graduate education in school psychology and a training program that includes at least 1,000 hours of experience supervised by a professional school psychologist, of which at least 500 hours must be in school settings. A specialist in school psychology provides psychological services under the supervision of a professional school psychologist.[6]

2. Titles for others who provide school psychological services under the supervision of a professional school psychologist may include *school psychological examiner, school psychological technician, school psychological assistant, school psychometrist,* or *school psychometric assistant.*

School psychological services refers to one or more of the following services offered to clients involved in educational settings, from preschool through higher education, for the protection and promotion of mental health and the facilitation of learning:[7]

A. Psychological and psychoeducational evaluation and assessment of the school functioning of children and young persons. Procedures include screening, psychological and educational tests (particularly individual psychological tests of intellectual functioning, cognitive development, affective behavior, and neuropsychological status), interviews, observation, and behavioral evaluations, with explicit regard for the context and setting in which the professional judgments based on assessment, diagnosis, and evaluation will be used.

B. Interventions to facilitate the functioning of individuals or groups, with concern for how schooling influences and is influenced by their cognitive, conative, affective, and social development. Such interventions may include, but are not limited to, recommending, planning, and evaluating special education services; psychoeducational therapy; counseling; affective educational programs; and training programs to improve coping skills.[8]

C. Interventions to facilitate the educational services and child care functions of school personnel, parents, and community agencies. Such interventions may include, but are not limited to, in-service school-personnel education programs, parent education programs, and parent counseling.

D. Consultation and collaboration with school personnel and/or parents concerning specific school-related problems of students and the professional problems of staff. Such services may include, but are not limited to, assistance with the planning of educational programs from a psychological perspective; consultation with teachers and other school personnel to enhance their understanding of the needs of particular pupils; modification of classroom instructional programs to facilitate children's learning; promotion of a positive climate for learning and teaching; assistance to parents to enable them to contribute to their children's development and school adjustment; and other staff development activities.

E. Program development services to individual schools, to school administrative systems, and to community agencies in such areas as needs assessment and evaluation of regular and special education programs; liaison with community, state, and federal agencies concerning the mental health and educational needs of children; coordination, administration, and planning of specialized educational programs; the generation, collection, organization, and dissemination of information from psychological research and theory to educate staff and parents.

F. Supervision of school psychological services (see Guideline 1.2, Interpretation).

A *school psychological service unit* is the functional unit through which school psychological services are provided; any such unit has at least one professional school psychologist associated with it:

A. Such a unit provides school psychological services to individuals, a school system, a district, a community agency, or a corporation, or to a consortium of school systems, districts, community agencies, or corporations that contract together to employ providers of school psychological services. A school psychological service unit is composed of one or more professional school psychologists and, in most instances, supporting psychological services staff.

B. A school psychological service unit may operate as an independent professional service to schools or as a functional component of an administrative organizational unit, such as a state department of education, a public or private school system, or a community mental health agency.

C. One or more professional school psychologists providing school psychological services in an interdisciplinary or a multidisciplinary setting constitute a school psychological service unit.

D. A school psychological service unit may also be one or more professional psychologists offering services in private practice, in a school psychological consulting firm, or in a college- or university-based facility or program that contracts to offer school psychological services to individuals, groups, school systems, districts, or corporations.

Users of school psychological services include:

A. Direct users or recipients of school psychological services, such as pupils, instructional and administrative school staff members, and parents.

B. Public and private institutions, facilities, or organizations receiving school psychological services, such as boards of education of public or private schools, mental health facilities, and other community agencies and educational institutions for handicapped or exceptional children.

C. Third-party purchasers—those who pay for the delivery of services but who are not the recipients of services.

D. Sanctioners—such as those who have a legitimate concern with the accessibility, timeliness, efficacy, and standards of quality attending the provision of school psychological services. Sanctioners may include members of the user's family, the court, the probation officer, the school administrator, the employer, the facility director, and so on. Sanctioners may also include various governmental, peer review, and accreditation bodies concerned with the assurance of quality.

Guideline 1
PROVIDERS

1.1 *Each school psychological service unit offering school psychological services has available at least one professional school psychologist and as many additional professional school psychologists and support personnel as are necessary to assure the adequacy and quality of services offered.*

INTERPRETATION: The intent of this Guideline is that one or more providers of psychological services in any school psychological service unit meet the levels of training and experience of the professional school psychologist specified in the preceding definitions.

When a professional school psychologist is not available on a full-time basis to provide school psychological services, the school district obtains the services of a professional school psychologist on a regular part-time basis. Yearly contracts are desirable to ensure continuity of services during a school year. The school psychologist so retained directs the psychological services, supervises the psychological services provided by support personnel, and participates sufficiently to be able to assess the need for services, review the content of services provided, and assume professional responsibility and accountability for them. A professional school psychologist supervises no more than the equivalent of 15 full-time specialists in school psychology and/or other school psychological personnel.

Districts that do not have easy access to professional school psychologists because of geographic considerations, or because professional school psychologists do not live or work in the area employ at least one full-time specialist in school psychology and as many more support personnel as are necessary to assure the adequacy and quality of services. The following strategies may be considered to acquire the necessary supervisory services from a professional school psychologist:

A. Employment by a county, region, consortium of schools, or state department of education of full-time supervisory personnel in school psychology who meet appropriate levels of training and experience, as specified in the definitions, to visit school districts regularly for supervision of psychological services staff.

B. Employment of professional school psychologists who engage in independent practice for the purpose of providing supervision to school district psychological services staff.

C. Arrangements with nearby school districts that employ professional school psychologists for part-time employment of such personnel on a contract basis specifically for the purpose of supervision as described in Guideline 1.

The school psychologist directing the school psychological service unit, whether on a full- or part-time basis, is responsible for determining and justifying appropriate ratios of school psychologists to users, to specialists in school psychology, and to support personnel, in order to ensure proper scope, accessibility, and quality of services provided in that setting. The school psychologist reports to the appropriate school district representatives any findings regarding the need to modify psychological services or staffing patterns to assure the adequacy and quality of services offered.

1.2 *Providers of school psychological services who do not meet the requirements for the professional school* *psychologist are supervised directly by a professional school psychologist who assumes professional responsibility and accountability for the services provided. The level and extent of supervision may vary from task to task so long as the supervising psychologist retains a sufficiently close supervisory relationship to meet this Guideline. Special proficiency training or supervision may be provided by a professional psychologist of another specialty or by a professional from another discipline whose competency in the given area has been demonstrated.*[9]

INTERPRETATION: Professional responsibility and accountability for the services provided require that the supervisor review reports and test protocols; review and discuss intervention strategies, plans, and outcomes; maintain a comprehensive view of the school's procedures and special concerns; and have sufficient opportunity to discuss discrepancies among the views of the supervisor, the supervised, and other school personnel on any problem or issue. In order to meet this Guideline, an appropriate number of hours per week are devoted to direct face-to-face supervision of each full-time school psychological service staff member. In no event is this supervision less than one hour per week for each staff member. The more comprehensive the psychological services are, the more supervision is needed. A plan or formula for relating increasing amounts of supervisory time to the complexity of professional responsibilities is to be developed. The amount and nature of supervision is specified in writing to all parties concerned.

1.3 *Wherever a school psychological service unit exists, a professional school psychologist is responsible for planning, directing, and reviewing the provision of school psychological services.*

INTERPRETATION: A school psychologist coordinates the activities of the school psychological service unit with other professionals, administrators, and community groups, both within and outside the school. This school psychologist, who may be the director, coordinator, or supervisor of the school psychological service unit, has related responsibilities including, but not limited to, recruiting qualified staff, directing training and research activities of the service, maintaining a high level of professional and ethical practice, and ensuring that staff members function only within the areas of their competency.

To facilitate the effectiveness of services by raising the level of staff sensitivity and professional skills, the psychologist designated as director is responsible for participating in the selection of staff and support personnel whose qualifications are directly relevant to the needs and characteristics of the users served.

In the event that a professional school psychologist is employed by the school psychological service unit on a basis that affords him or her insufficient time to carry out full responsibility for coordinating or directing the unit, a specialist in school psychology is designated as

director or coordinator of the school psychological services and is supervised by a professional school psychologist employed on a part-time basis, for a minimum of 2 hours per week.

1.4 *When functioning as part of an organizational setting, professional school psychologists bring their backgrounds and skills to bear on the goals of the organization, whenever appropriate, by participating in the planning and development of overall services.*

INTERPRETATION: Professional school psychologists participate in the maintenance of high professional standards by serving as representatives on, or consultants to, committees and boards concerned with service delivery, especially when such committees deal with special education, pupil personnel services, mental health aspects of schooling, or other services that use or involve school psychological knowledge and skills.

As appropriate to the setting, school psychologists' activities may include active participation, as voting and as office-holding members, on the facility's executive, planning, and evaluation boards and committees.

1.5 *School psychologists maintain current knowledge of scientific and professional developments to preserve and enhance their professional competence.*

INTERPRETATION: Methods through which knowledge of scientific and professional developments may be gained include, but are not limited to, (a) the reading or preparation of scientific and professional publications and other materials, (b) attendance at workshops and presentations at meetings and conventions, (c) participation in on-the-job staff development programs, and (d) other forms of continuing education. The school psychologist and staff have available reference material and journals related to the provision of school psychological services. School psychologists are prepared to show evidence periodically that they are staying abreast of current knowledge in the field of school psychology and are also keeping their certification and licensing credentials up-to-date.

1.6 *School psychologists limit their practice to their demonstrated areas of professional competence.*

INTERPRETATION: School psychological services are offered in accordance with the providers' areas of competence as defined by verifiable training and experience. When extending services beyond the range of their usual practice, school psychologists obtain pertinent training or appropriate professional supervision. Such training or supervision is consistent with the extension of functions performed and services provided. An extension of services may involve a change in the theoretical orientation of the practitioner, in the techniques used, in the client age group (e.g., children, adolescents, or parents), or in the kinds of problems addressed (e.g., mental retardation, neurological impairment, learning disabilities, family relationships).

1.7 *Psychologists who wish to qualify as school psychologists meet the same requirements with respect to subject matter and professional skills that apply to doctoral training in school psychology.*[10]

INTERPRETATION: Education of psychologists to qualify them for specialty practice in school psychology is under the auspices of a department in a regionally accredited university or of a professional school that offers the doctoral degree in school psychology, through campus- and/or field-based arrangements. Such education is individualized, with due credit being given for relevant course work and other requirements that have previously been satisfied. In addition to the doctoral-level education specified above, appropriate doctoral-level training is required. An internship or experience in a school setting is not adequate preparation for becoming a school psychologist when prior education has not been in that area. Fulfillment of such an individualized training program is attested to by the awarding of a certificate by the supervising department or professional school that indicates the successful completion of preparation in school psychology.

1.8 *Professional school psychologists are encouraged to develop innovative theories and procedures and to provide appropriate theoretical and/or empirical support for their innovations.*

INTERPRETATION: A specialty of a profession rooted in science intends continually to explore, study, and conduct research with a view to developing and verifying new and improved methods of serving the school population in ways that can be documented.

Guideline 2
PROGRAMS

2.1 *Composition and organization of a school psychological service unit:*

2.1.1 *The composition and programs of a school psychological service unit are responsive to the needs of the school population that is served.*

INTERPRETATION: A school psychological service unit is structured so as to facilitate effective and economical delivery of services. For example, a school psychological service unit serving predominantly low-income, ethnic, or racial minority children has a staffing pattern and service programs that are adapted to the linguistic, experiential, and attitudinal characteristics of the users. Appropriate types of assessment materials and norm ref-

erence groups are utilized in the practice of school psychology.

2.1.2 *A description of the organization of the school psychological service unit and its lines of responsibility and accountability for the delivery of school psychological services is available in written form to instructional and administrative staff of the unit and to parents, students, and members of the community.*

INTERPRETATION: The description includes lines of responsibility, supervisory relationships, and the level and extent of accountability for each person who provides school psychological services.

2.1.3 *A school psychological service unit includes sufficient numbers of professional and support personnel to achieve its goals, objectives, and purposes.*

INTERPRETATION: A school psychological service unit includes one or more professional school psychologists, specialists in school psychology, and other psychological services support personnel. When a professional school psychologist is not available to provide services on a full- or part-time basis, the school psychological services are conducted by a specialist in school psychology, supervised by a professional school psychologist (see Guideline 1.2).

The work load and diversity of school psychological services required and the specific goals and objectives of the setting determine the numbers and qualifications of professional and support personnel in the school psychological service unit. For example, the extent to which services involve case study, direct intervention, and/or consultation will be significant in any service plan. Case study frequently involves teacher and/or parent conferences, observations of pupils, and a multi-assessment review, including student interviews. Similarly, the target populations for services affect the range of services that can be offered. One school psychologist, or one specialist in school psychology under supervision, for every 2,000 pupils is considered appropriate.[11]

Where shortages in personnel exist, so that school psychological services cannot be rendered in a professional manner, the director of the school psychological service unit informs the supervisor/administrator of the service about the implications of the shortage and initiates action to remedy the situation. When this fails, the director appropriately modifies the scope or work load of the unit to maintain the quality of services rendered.

2.2 *Policies:*

2.2.1 *When the school psychological service unit is composed of more than one person or is a component of a larger organization, a written statement of its objectives and scope of services is developed, maintained, and reviewed.*

INTERPRETATION: The school psychological service unit reviews its objectives and scope of services annually and revises them as necessary to ensure that the school psychological services offered are consistent with staff competencies and current psychological knowledge and practice. This statement is discussed with staff, reviewed by the appropriate administrators, distributed to instructional and administrative staff and school board members, and when appropriate, made available to parents, students, and members of the community upon request.

2.2.2 *All providers within a school psychological service unit support the legal and civil rights of the users.*[12]

INTERPRETATION: Providers of school psychological services safeguard the interests of school personnel, students, and parents with regard to personal, legal, and civil rights. They are continually sensitive to the issue of confidentiality of information, the short-term and long-term impacts of their decisions and recommendations, and other matters pertaining to individual, legal, and civil rights. Concerns regarding the safeguarding of individual rights of school personnel, students, and parents include, but are not limited to, due-process rights of parents and children, problems of self-incrimination in judicial proceedings, involuntary commitment to hospitals, child abuse, freedom of choice, protection of minors or legal incompetents, discriminatory practices in identification and placement, recommendations for special education provisions, and adjudication of domestic relations disputes in divorce and custodial proceedings. Providers of school psychological services take affirmative action by making themselves available to local committees, review boards, and similar advisory groups established to safeguard the human, civil, and legal rights of children and parents.

2.2.3 *All providers within a school psychological service unit are familiar with and adhere to the American Psychological Association's* Standards for Providers of Psychological Services, Ethical Principles of Psychologists, Standards for Educational and Psychological Tests, Ethical Principles in the Conduct of Research With Human Participants, *and other official policy statements relevant to standards for professional services issued by the Association.*

INTERPRETATION: A copy of each of these documents is maintained by providers of school psychological services and is available upon request to all school personnel and officials, parents, members of the community, and where applicable, students and other sanctioners.

2.2.4 *All providers within a school psychological service unit conform to relevant statutes established by federal, state, and local governments.*

INTERPRETATION: All providers of school psychological services are familiar with and conform to appropriate statutes regulating the practice of psychology. They also are informed about state department of education requirements and other agency regulations that have the force of law and that relate to the delivery of school psychological services (e.g., certification of, eligibility for, and placement in, special education programs). In addition, all providers are cognizant that federal agencies such as the Department of Education and the Department of Health and Human Services have policy statements regarding psychological services. Providers of school psychological services are familiar as well with other statutes and regulations, including those addressed to the civil and legal rights of users (e.g., Public Law 94-142, The Education for All Handicapped Children Act of 1975), that are pertinent to their scope of practice.

It is the responsibility of the American Psychological Association to maintain files of those federal policies, statutes, and regulations relating to this section and to assist its members in obtaining them. The state psychological associations, school psychological associations, and state licensing boards periodically publish and distribute appropriate state statutes and regulations.

2.2.5 *All providers within a school psychological service unit inform themselves about and use the network of human services in their communities in order to link users with relevant services and resources.*

INTERPRETATION: School psychologists and support staff are sensitive to the broader context of human needs. In recognizing the matrix of personal and societal problems, providers make available to clients information regarding human services such as legal aid societies, social services, health resources like mental health centers, private practitioners, and educational and recreational facilities. School psychological staff formulate and maintain a file of such resources for reference. The specific information provided is such that users can easily make contact with the services and freedom of choice can be honored. Providers of school psychological services refer to such community resources and, when indicated, actively intervene on behalf of the users. School psychologists seek opportunities to serve on boards of community agencies in order to represent the needs of the school population in the community.

2.2.6 *In the delivery of school psychological services, providers maintain a cooperative relationship with colleagues and co-workers in the best interest of the users.*

INTERPRETATION: School psychologists recognize the areas of special competence of other psychologists and of other professionals in the school and in the community for either consultation or referral purposes (e.g., school social workers, speech therapists, remedial reading teachers, special education teachers, pediatricians, neurologists, and public health nurses). Providers of school psychological services make appropriate use of other professional, research, technical, and administrative resources whenever these serve the best interests of the school staff, children, and parents and establish and maintain cooperative and/or collaborative arrangements with such other resources as required to meet the needs of users.

2.3 Procedures:

2.3.1 *A school psychological service unit follows a set of procedural guidelines for the delivery of school psychological services.*

INTERPRETATION: The school psychological service staff is prepared to provide a statement of procedural guidelines in written form in terms that can be understood by school staff, parents, school board members, interested members of the community, and when appropriate, students and other sanctioners. The statement describes the current methods, forms, case study and assessment procedures, estimated time lines, interventions, and evaluation techniques being used to achieve the objectives and goals for school psychological services.

This statement is communicated to school staff and personnel, school board members, parents, and when appropriate, students or other sanctioners through whatever means are feasible, including in-service activities, conferences, oral presentations, and dissemination of written materials.

The school psychological service unit provides for the annual review of its procedures for the delivery of school psychological services.

2.3.2 *Providers of school psychological services develop plans appropriate to the providers' professional practices and to the problems presented by the users. There is a mutually acceptable understanding between providers and school staff, parents, and students or responsible agents regarding the goals and the delivery of services.*

INTERPRETATION: The school psychological service unit notifies the school unit in writing of the plan that is adopted for use and resolves any points of difference. The plan includes written consent of guardians of students and, when appropriate, consent of students for the services provided. Similarly, the nature of the assessment tools that are to be used and the reasons for their inclusion are spelled out. The objectives of intervention(s) of a psychological nature as well as the procedures for implementing the intervention(s) are specified. An estimate of time is noted where appropriate. Parents and/or students are made aware of the various decisions that can be made as a result of the service(s), participate in accounting for decisions that are made, and are informed of how appeals may be instituted.

2.3.3 *Accurate, current, and pertinent documentation of essential school psychological services provided is maintained.*

INTERPRETATION: Records kept of psychological services may include, but are not limited to, identifying data, dates of services, names of providers of services, types of services, and significant actions taken. These records are maintained separately from the child's cumulative record folder. Once a case study is completed and/or an intervention begun, records are reviewed and updated at least monthly.

2.3.4 *Each school psychological services unit follows an established record retention and disposition policy.*

INTERPRETATION: The policy on maintenance and review of psychological records (including the length of time that records not already part of school records are to be kept) is developed by the local school psychological service unit. This policy is consistent with existing federal and state statutes and regulations.

2.3.5 *Providers of school psychological services maintain a system to protect confidentiality of their records.*

INTERPRETATION: School psychologists are responsible for maintaining the confidentiality of information about users of services, from whatever source derived. All persons supervised by school psychologists, including nonprofessional personnel and students, who have access to records of psychological services maintain this confidentiality as a condition of employment. All appropriate staff receive training regarding the confidentiality of records.

Users are informed in advance of any limits for maintenance of confidentiality of psychological information. Procedures for obtaining informed consent are developed by the school psychological service unit. Written informed consent is obtained to conduct assessment or to carry out psychological intervention services. Informing users of the manner in which requests for information will be handled and of the school personnel who will share the results is part of the process of obtaining consent.

The school psychologist conforms to current laws and regulations with respect to the release of confidential information. As a general rule, however, the school psychologist does not release confidential information, except with the written consent of the parent or, where appropriate, the student directly involved or his or her legal representative. Even after consent for release has been obtained, the school psychologist clearly identifies such information as confidential to the recipient of the information. When there is a conflict with a statute, with regulations with the force of law, or with a court order, the school psychologist seeks a resolution to the conflict that is both ethically and legally feasible and appropriate.

Providers of school psychological services ensure that psychological reports which will become part of the school records are reviewed carefully so that confidentiality of pupils and parents is protected. When the guardian or student intends to waive confidentiality, the school psychologist discusses the implications of releasing psychological information and assists the user in limiting disclosure to only that information required by the present circumstance.

Raw psychological data (e.g., test protocols, counseling or interview notes, or questionnaires) in which a user is identified are released only with the written consent of the user or his or her legal representative, or by court order when such material is not covered by legal confidentiality, and are released only to a person recognized by the school psychologist as competent to use the data.

Any use made of psychological reports, records, or data for research or training purposes is consistent with this Guideline. Additionally, providers of school psychological services comply with statutory confidentiality requirements and those embodied in the American Psychological Association's *Ethical Principles of Psychologists* (APA, 1981).

Providers of school psychological services remain sensitive to both the benefits and the possible misuse of information regarding individuals that is stored in large computerized data banks. Providers use their influence to ensure that such information is managed in a socially responsible manner.

Guideline 3
ACCOUNTABILITY

3.1 *The promotion of human welfare is the primary principle guiding the professional activity of the school psychologist and the school psychological service unit.*

INTERPRETATION: School psychological services staff provide services to school staff members, students, and parents in a manner that is considerate and effective.

School psychologists make their services readily accessible to users in a manner that facilitates the users' freedom of choice. Parents, students, and other users are made aware that psychological services may be available through other public or private sources, and relevant information for exercising such options is provided upon request.

School psychologists are mindful of their accountability to the administration, to the school board, and to the general public, provided that appropriate steps are taken to protect the confidentiality of the service relationship. In the pursuit of their professional activities, they aid in the conservation of human, material, and financial resources.

The school psychological service unit does not withhold services to children or parents on the basis of the users' race, color, religion, gender, sexual orientation, age, or national origin. Recognition is given, however, to the following considerations: (a) the professional right of school psychologists, at the time of their employment, to state that they wish to limit their services to a specific category of users (e.g., elementary school children, exceptional children, adolescents), noting their reasons so

that employers can make decisions regarding their employment, assignment of their duties, and so on; (b) the right and responsibility of school psychologists to withhold an assessment procedure when not validly applicable; (c) the right and responsibility of school psychologists to withhold evaluative, psychotherapeutic, counseling, or other services in specific instances in which their own limitations or client characteristics might impair the effectiveness of the relationship; and (d) the obligation of school psychologists to seek to ameliorate through peer review, consultation, or other personal therapeutic procedures those factors that inhibit the provision of services to particular users. In such instances, it is incumbent on school psychologists to advise clients about appropriate alternative services. When appropriate services are not available, school psychologists inform the school district administration and/or other sanctioners of the unmet needs of clients. In all instances, school psychologists make available information, and provide opportunity to participate in decisions, concerning such issues as initiation, termination, continuation, modification, and evaluation of psychological services. These Guidelines are also made available upon request.

Accurate and full information is made available to prospective individual or organizational users regarding the qualifications of providers, the nature and extent of services offered, and where appropriate, the financial costs as well as the benefits and possible risks of the proposed services.

Professional school psychologists offering services for a fee inform users of their payment policies, if applicable, and of their willingness to assist in obtaining reimbursement when such services have been contracted for as an external resource.

3.2 *School psychologists pursue their activities as members of the independent, autonomous profession of psychology.*[13]

INTERPRETATION: School psychologists are aware of the implications of their activities for the profession of psychology as a whole. They seek to eliminate discriminatory practices instituted for self-serving purposes that are not in the interest of the users (e.g., arbitrary requirements for referral and supervision by another profession) and to discourage misuse of psychological concepts and tools (e.g., use of psychological instruments for special education placement by school personnel or others who lack relevant and adequate education and training). School psychologists are cognizant of their responsibilities for the development of the profession and for the improvement of schools. They participate where possible in the training and career development of students and other providers; they participate as appropriate in the training of school administrators, teachers, and paraprofessionals; and they integrate, and supervise the implementation of, their contributions within the structure established for delivering school psychological services. Where appropriate, they facilitate the development of, and participate in, professional standards review mechanisms.

School psychologists seek to work with other professionals in a cooperative manner for the good of the users and the benefit of the general public. School psychologists associated with special education or mental health teams or with multidisciplinary settings support the principle that members of each participating profession have equal rights and opportunities to share all privileges and responsibilities of full membership in the educational or human service activities or facilities and to administer service programs in their respective areas of competence. (Refer also to Guideline 2.2.5, Interpretation.)

3.3 *There are periodic, systematic, and effective evaluations of school psychological services.*

INTERPRETATION: When the psychological service unit representing school psychology is a component of a larger organization (e.g., school system, county or state regional district, state department of education), regular evaluation of progress in achieving goals is provided for in the service delivery plan, including consideration of the effectiveness of school psychological services relative to costs in terms of use of time and money and the availability of professional and support personnel.

Evaluation of the school psychological service delivery system is conducted internally and, when possible, under independent auspices as well. This evaluation includes an assessment of effectiveness (to determine what the service unit accomplished), efficiency (to determine the costs of providing the services), continuity (to ensure that the services are appropriately linked to other educational services), availability (to determine the appropriateness of staffing ratios), accessibility (to ensure that the services are readily available to members of the school population), and adequacy (to determine whether the services meet the identified needs of the school population).

It is highly desirable that there be a periodic reexamination of review mechanisms to ensure that these attempts at public safeguards are effective and cost efficient and do not place unnecessary encumbrances on the providers or impose unnecessary expenses on users or sanctioners for services rendered.

3.4 *School psychologists are accountable for all aspects of the services they provide and are responsive to those concerned with these services.*

INTERPRETATION: In recognizing their responsibilities to users, sanctioners, and other providers, and where appropriate and consistent with the users' legal rights and privileged communications, school psychologists make available information about, and provide opportunity to participate in, decisions concerning such issues as initiation, termination, continuation, modification, and evaluation of school psychological services.

Guideline 4
ENVIRONMENT

4.1 *Providers of psychological services promote development in the school setting of a physical, organizational, and social environment that facilitates optimal human functioning.*

INTERPRETATION: Federal, state, and local requirements for safety, health, and sanitation are observed.

As providers of services, school psychologists are concerned with the environment of their service units, especially as it affects the quality of service, but also as it impinges on human functioning in the school. Attention is given to the privacy and comfort of school staff, students, and parents. Parent and staff interviews are conducted in a professional atmosphere, with the option for private conferences available. Students are seen under conditions that maximize their privacy and enhance the possibility for meaningful intervention; for example, they should have the opportunity to leave their classroom inconspicuously and should be free from interruptions when meeting with the psychologist. Physical arrangements and organizational policies and procedures are conducive to the human dignity, self-respect, and optimal functioning of school staff, students, and parents and to the effective delivery of service.

FOOTNOTES

[1] The footnotes appended to these Specialty Guidelines represent an attempt to provide a coherent context of earlier APA policy statements and other documents regarding professional practice. The Guidelines extend these previous policy statements where necessary to reflect current concerns of the public and the profession.

[2] There are three categories of individuals who do not meet the definition of *professional school psychologist* but who can be considered professional school psychologists if they meet certain criteria.

The following two categories of professional psychologists who met the criteria indicated below on or before the adoption of these Specialty Guidelines on January 31, 1980, are considered professional school psychologists: Category 1—those who completed (a) a doctoral degree program primarily psychological in content, but not in school psychology, at a regionally accredited university or professional school and (b) 3 postdoctoral years of appropriate education, training, and experience in providing school psychological services as defined herein, including a minimum of 1,200 hours in school settings; Category 2—those who on or before September 4, 1974, (a) completed a master's degree from a program primarily psychological in content at a regionally accredited university or professional school and (b) held a license or certificate in the state in which they practiced, conferred by a state board of psychological examiners, or the endorsement of a state psychological association through voluntary certification, and who, in addition, prior to January 31, 1980, (c) obtained 5 post-master's years of appropriate education, training, and experience in providing school psychological services as defined herein, including a minimum of 2,400 hours in school settings.

After January 31, 1980, professional psychologists who wish

42

to be recognized as professional school psychologists are referred to Guideline 1.7.

The APA Council of Representatives passed a "Resolution on the Master's-Level Issue" in January 1977 containing the following statement, which influenced the development of a third category of professional school psychologists:

> The title "Professional Psychologist" has been used so widely and by persons with such a wide variety of training and experience that it does not provide the information the public deserves.
>
> As a consequence, the APA takes the position and makes it a part of its policy that the use of the title "Professional Psychologist," and its variations such as "Clinical Psychologist," "Counseling Psychologist," "School Psychologist," and "Industrial Psychologist" are reserved for those who have completed a Doctoral Training Program in Psychology in a university, college, or professional school of psychology that is APA or regionally accredited. In order to meet this standard, a transition period will be acknowledged for the use of the title "School Psychologist," so that ways may be sought to increase opportunities for doctoral training and to improve the level of educational codes pertaining to the title. (Conger, 1977, p. 426)

For the purpose of transition, then, there is still another category of persons who can be considered professional school psychologists for practice in elementary and secondary schools. Category 3 consists of persons who meet the following criteria on or before, but not beyond, January 31, 1985: (a) a master's or higher degree, requiring at least 2 years of full-time graduate study in school psychology, from a regionally accredited university or professional school; (b) at least 3 additional years of training and experience in school psychological services, including a minimum of 1,200 hours in school settings; and (c) a license or certificate conferred by a state board of psychological examiners or a state educational agency for practice in elementary or secondary schools.

Preparation equivalent to that described in Category 3 entitles an individual to use the title *professional school psychologist* in school practice, but it does not exempt the individual from meeting the requirements of licensure or other requirements for which a doctoral degree is prerequisite.

[3] A professional school psychologist who is licensed by a state or District of Columbia board of examiners of psychology for the independent practice of psychology and who has 2 years of supervised (or equivalent) experience in health services, of which at least 1 year is postdoctoral, may be listed as a "Health Service Provider in Psychology" in the *National Register of Health Service Providers in Psychology*:

> A Health Service Provider in Psychology is defined as a psychologist, certified/licensed at the independent practice level in his/her state, who is duly trained and experienced in the delivery of direct, preventive, assessment and therapeutic intervention services to individuals whose growth, adjustment, or functioning is actually impaired or is demonstrably at high risk of impairment. (Council for the National Register of Health Service Providers in Psychology, 1980, p. xi)

[4] The areas of knowledge and training that are a part of the educational program for all professional psychologists have been presented in two APA documents, *Education and Credentialing in Psychology II* (APA, 1977a) and *Criteria for Accreditation of Doctoral Training Programs and Internships in Professional Psychology* (APA, 1979). There is consistency in the presentation of core areas in the education and training of all professional psychologists. The description of education and training in these Guidelines is based primarily on the document *Education and Credentialing in Psychology II*. It is intended to indicate broad areas of required curriculum, with the expectation that training programs will undoubtedly want to interpret the specific content of these areas in different ways depending on the nature, philosophy, and intent of the programs.

[5] Although specialty education and training guidelines have not yet been developed and approved by APA, the following description of education and training components of school psychology programs represents a consensus regarding specialty training in school psychology at this time.

The *education* of school psychologists encompasses the equivalent of at least 3 years of full-time graduate academic study. While instructional formats and course titles may vary from program to program, each program has didactic and experiential instruction (a) in scientific and professional areas common to all professional psychology programs, such as ethics and standards, research design and methodology, statistics, and psychometric methods, and (b) in such substantive areas as the biological bases of behavior, the cognitive and affective bases of behavior, the social, cultural, ethnic, and sex role bases of behavior, and individual differences. Course work includes social and philosophical bases of education, curriculum theory and practice, etiology of learning and behavior disorders, exceptional children, and special education. Organization theory and administrative practice should also be included in the program. This list is not intended to dictate specific courses or a sequence of instruction. It is the responsibility of programs to determine how these areas are organized and presented to students. Variations in educational format are to be expected.

The *training* of school psychologists includes practicum and field experience in conjunction with the educational program. In addition, the program includes a supervised internship experience beyond practicum and field work, equivalent to at least 1 academic school year, but in no event fewer than 1,200 hours, in schools or in a combination of schools and community agencies and centers, with at least 600 hours of the internship in the school setting. An appropriate number of hours per week should be devoted to direct face-to-face supervision of each intern. In no event is there less than 1 hour per week of direct supervision. Overall professional supervision is provided by a professional school psychologist. However, supervision in specific procedures and techniques may be provided by others, with the agreement of the supervising professional psychologist and the supervisee. The training experiences provided and the competencies developed occur in settings in which there are opportunities to work with children, teachers, and parents and to supervise others providing psychological services to children.

[6] In order to implement these Specialty Guidelines, it will be necessary to determine in each state which non-doctoral-level school psychologists certified by the state department of education are eligible to be considered professional school psychologists for practice in elementary and secondary schools. A national register of all professional school psychologists and specialists in school psychology would be a useful and efficient means by which to inform the public of the available school psychological services personnel.

[7] Functions and activities of school psychologists relating to the teaching of psychology, the writing or editing of scholarly or scientific manuscripts, and the conduct of scientific research do not fall within the purview of these Guidelines.

[8] Nothing in these Guidelines precludes the school psychologist from being trained beyond the areas described herein (e.g., in psychotherapy for children, adolescents, and their families in relation to school-related functioning and problems) and, therefore, from providing services on the basis of this training to clients as appropriate.

[9] In some states, a supervisor's certificate is required in order to use the title *supervisor* in the public schools. Supervision of providers of psychological services by a professional school psy-

chologist does not mean that the school psychologist is thereby authorized or entitled to offer supervision to other school personnel. Supervision by the school psychologist is confined to those areas appropriate to his or her training and educational background and is viewed as part of the school psychologist's professional responsibilities and duties.

The following guideline for supervision has been written by the Executive Committee of the Division of School Psychology:

> In addition to being a professional school psychologist, the person who supervises school psychological services and/or school psychological personnel shall have the following qualifications: broad understanding of diagnostic assessment, consultation, programming, and other intervention strategies; skills in supervision; the ability to empathize with supervisees; and commitment to continuing education. The supervising school psychologist also shall have had the equivalent of at least 2 years of satisfactory full-time, on-the-job experience as a school psychologist practicing directly in the school or dealing with school-related problems in independent practice.

[10] This Guideline follows closely the statement regarding "Policy on Training for Psychologists Wishing to Change Their Specialty" adopted by the APA Council of Representatives in January 1976. Included therein was the implementing provision that "this policy statement shall be incorporated in the guidelines of the Committee on Accreditation so that appropriate sanctions can be brought to bear on university and internship training programs that violate [it]" (Conger, 1976, p. 424).

[11] Two surveys of school psychological practice provide a rationale for the specification of this Guideline (Farling & Hoedt, 1971; Kicklighter, 1976). The median ratios of psychologists to pupils were 1 to 9,000 in 1966 and 1 to 4,000 in 1974. Those responding to Kicklighter's survey projected that the ratio of psychologists to pupils would be 1 to 2,500 in 1980. These data were collected before the passage of Public Law 94-142, the Education for All Handicapped Children Act of 1975. The regulations for implementing this act require extensive identification, assessment, and evaluation services to children, and it is reasonable in 1981 to set an acceptable ratio of psychologists to pupils at 1 to 2,000.

[12] See also Ethical Principles of Psychologists (APA, 1981), especially Principles 5 (Confidentiality), 6 (Welfare of the Consumer), and 9 (Research With Human Participants), and Ethical Principles in the Conduct of Research With Human Participants (APA, 1973). Also, in 1978 Division 17 approved in principle a statement on "Principles for Counseling and Psychotherapy With Women," which was designed to protect the interests of female users of counseling psychological services.

[13] Support for the principle of the independence of psychology as a profession is found in the following:

> As a member of an autonomous profession, a psychologist rejects limitations upon his [or her] freedom of thought and action other than those imposed by his [or her] moral, legal, and social responsibilities. The Association is always prepared to provide appropriate assistance to any responsible member who becomes subjected to unreasonable limitations upon his [or her] opportunity to function as a practitioner, teacher, researcher, administrator, or consultant. The Association is always prepared to cooperate with any responsible profes-

sional organization in opposing any unreasonable limitations on the professional functions of the members of that organization.

> This insistence upon professional autonomy has been upheld over the years by the affirmative actions of the courts and other public and private bodies in support of the right of the psychologist—and other professionals—to pursue those functions for which he [or she] is trained and qualified to perform. (APA, 1968, p. 9)

> Organized psychology has the responsibility to define and develop its own profession, consistent with the general canons of science and with the public welfare.

> Psychologists recognize that other professions and other groups will, from time to time, seek to define the roles and responsibilities of psychologists. The APA opposes such developments on the same principle that it is opposed to the psychological profession taking positions which would define the work and scope of responsibility of other duly recognized professions. (APA, 1972, p. 333)

REFERENCES

American Psychological Association. *Psychology as a profession*. Washington, D.C.: Author, 1968.

American Psychological Association. Guidelines for conditions of employment of psychologists. *American Psychologist*, 1972, *27*, 331–334.

American Psychological Association. *Ethical principles in the conduct of research with human participants*. Washington, D.C.: Author, 1973.

American Psychological Association. *Standards for educational and psychological tests*. Washington, D.C.: Author, 1974. (a)

American Psychological Association. *Standards for providers of psychological services*. Washington, D.C.: Author, 1974. (b)

American Psychological Association. *Education and credentialing in psychology II*. Report of a meeting, June 4–5, 1977. Washington, D.C.: Author, 1977. (a)

American Psychological Association. *Standards for providers of psychological services* (Rev. ed.). Washington, D.C.: Author, 1977. (b)

American Psychological Association. *Criteria for accreditation of doctoral training programs and internships in professional psychology*. Washington, D.C.: Author, 1979 (amended 1980).

American Psychological Association. *Ethical principles of psychologists* (Rev. ed.). Washington, D.C.: Author, 1981.

Conger, J. J. Proceedings of the American Psychological Association, Incorporated, for the year 1975: Minutes of the annual meeting of the Council of Representatives. *American Psychologist*, 1976, *31*, 406–434.

Conger, J. J. Proceedings of the American Psychological Association, Incorporated, for the year 1976: Minutes of the annual meeting of the Council of Representatives. *American Psychologist*, 1977, *32*, 408–438.

Council for the National Register of Health Service Providers in Psychology. *National register of health service providers in psychology*. Washington, D.C.: Author, 1980.

Farling, W. H., & Hoedt, K. C. *National survey of school psychologists*. Washington, D.C.: Department of Health, Education, and Welfare, 1971.

Kicklighter, R. H. School psychology in the U.S.: A quantitative survey. *Journal of School Psychology*, 1976, *14*, 151–156.